Biodiversity and Conservation

Other Books in the Global Viewpoints Series

GLOBALVIEWPOINTS

Biodiversity and Conservation

Lisa Idzikowski, Book Editor

GREENHAVEN
PUBLISHING

Published in 2020 by Greenhaven Publishing, LLC
353 3rd Avenue, Suite 255, New York, NY 10010

Copyright © 2020 by Greenhaven Publishing, LLC

First Edition

Articles in Greenhaven Publishing anthologies are often edited for length to meet page
requirements. In addition, original titles of these works are changed to clearly present
the main thesis and to explicitly indicate the author's opinion. Every effort is made to
ensure that Greenhaven Publishing accurately reflects the original intent of the authors.
Every effort has been made to trace the owners of the copyrighted material.

Cover image: Ethan Daniels/Shutterstock.com, © Can Stock Photo/
Volokhatiuk (clouds), © Tsiumpa/Dreamstime.com (earth)

Map: frees/Shutterstock.com

Library of Congress Cataloging-in-Publication Data

Names: Idzikowski, Lisa, editor.
Title: Biodiversity and conservation / Lisa Idzikowski, book editor.
Description: First edition. | New York : Greenhaven Publishing, 2020. | Series: Global
viewpoints | Includes bibliographical references and index. | Audience: Grades 9–12.
Identifiers: LCCN 2019022601 | ISBN 9781534506411 (library
binding) | ISBN 9781534506404 (paperback)
Subjects: LCSH: Biodiversity conservation—Juvenile literature.
Classification: LCC QH75 .B528 2020 | DDC 333.95/16—dc23
LC record available at https://lccn.loc.gov/2019022601

Manufactured in the United States of America

Website: http://greenhavenpublishing.com

Contents

Chapter 2: What Causes the Loss of Biodiversity?

Farmers around the world see themselves as stewards of the land. Many use up-to-date techniques supported by research to decrease problems such as erosion on their lands. These practices also work to increase biological diversity.

Chapter 3: Why Is Biodiversity Important for Human Survival?

spent in nature, which is vital for physical and emotional
health.

Chapter 4: How Can Biodiversity Be Preserved?

This research shows it is possible to reclaim land disturbed by human use.

Foreword

"The problems of all of humanity can
only be solved by all of humanity."
—Swiss author Friedrich Dürrenmatt

Global interdependence has become an undeniable reality. Mass media and technology have increased worldwide access to information and created a society of global citizens. Understanding and navigating this global community is a challenge, requiring a high degree of information literacy and a new level of learning sophistication.

Building on the success of its flagship series, Opposing Viewpoints, Greenhaven Publishing has created the Global Viewpoints series to examine a broad range of current, often controversial topics of worldwide importance from a variety of international perspectives. Providing students and other readers with the information they need to explore global connections and think critically about worldwide implications, each Global Viewpoints volume offers a panoramic view of a topic of widespread significance.

Drugs, famine, immigration—a broad, international treatment is essential to do justice to social, environmental, health, and political issues such as these. Junior high, high school, and early college students, as well as general readers, can all use Global Viewpoints anthologies to discern the complexities relating to each issue. Readers will be able to examine unique national perspectives while, at the same time, appreciating the interconnectedness that global priorities bring to all nations and cultures.

Material in each volume is selected from a diverse range of sources, including journals, magazines, newspapers, nonfiction books, speeches, government documents, pamphlets, organization newsletters, and position papers. Global Viewpoints is truly global, with material drawn primarily from international sources available in English and secondarily from U.S. sources with extensive international coverage.

Features of each volume in the Global Viewpoints series include:

- An **annotated table of contents** that provides a brief summary of each essay in the volume, including the name of the country or area covered in the essay.

- An **introduction** specific to the volume topic.

- A world map to help readers locate the countries or areas covered in the essays.

- For each viewpoint, **an introduction** that contains notes about the author and source of the viewpoint explains why material from the specific country is being presented, summarizes the main points of the viewpoint, and offers three **guided reading questions** to aid in understanding and comprehension.

- **For further discussion** questions that promote critical thinking by asking the reader to compare and contrast aspects of the viewpoints or draw conclusions about perspectives and arguments.

- A worldwide list of **organizations to contact** for readers seeking additional information.

- A **periodical bibliography** for each chapter and a **bibliography of books** on the volume topic to aid in further research.

- A comprehensive **subject index** to offer access to people, places, events, and subjects cited in the text.

Global Viewpoints is designed for a broad spectrum of readers who want to learn more about current events, history, political science, government, international relations, economics, environmental science, world cultures, and sociology— students doing research for class assignments or debates, teachers and faculty seeking to supplement course materials, and others wanting to understand current issues better. By presenting how people in various countries perceive the root causes, current consequences, and proposed solutions to worldwide challenges, Global Viewpoints volumes offer readers opportunities to enhance their global awareness and their knowledge of cultures worldwide.

Introduction

> *"Unlike the rest of science, the study of biodiversity has a time limit. Species are disappearing at an accelerating rate through human action, primarily habitat destruction but also pollution and the introduction of exotic species into residual natural environments. I have said that a fifth or more of the species of plants and animals could vanish or be doomed to early extinction by the year 2020 unless better efforts are made to save them."*
>
> *—E.O. Wilson,*
> *Professor Emeritus and*
> *Environmental Scientist*

Biodiversity is a topic on the minds of many these days. Scientists, college students, CEO's, professors, parents and children, neighbors—even the Pope. Almost everywhere you turn, people are talking about the extinction of species, how to avoid plastic pollution getting into the oceans, rainforest deforestation, taking care of the Earth and its ecosystems, invasive species, overconsumption, and the list goes on. And if they're not talking about this, they should be.

According to the World Wildlife Fund, "Biodiversity is all the different kinds of life you'll find in one area—the variety of animals, plants, fungi, and even microorganisms like bacteria that make up our natural world." Everything is important, and "each of these species and organisms work together in ecosystems, like an intricate web, to maintain balance and support life." Now many people might immediately think about the elephants, lions, and polar bears that they hear about and the fact that these large, showy, creatures are disappearing. But like the too small to see with the naked eye bacteria and microorganisms, and even bugs that people love to hate, biodiversity encompasses all other living things and "supports everything in nature that we need to survive: food, clean water, medicine, and shelter."

It's both scary and hard to believe that some powerful individuals, including politicians, and countries don't seem to care about or take seriously the dire warnings from scientists and researchers regarding threats to our biodiversity. How many species of animals and plants will be gone forever before these individuals come to their senses? How many potential new medicines won't be discovered because the wild plants that form them will be already extinct? Or how much of the tropical rainforest that supports the planet's need for oxygen will be already clear cut?

US president Donald Trump is a good example. He, his administration, and his business associates are hard at work supporting changes to legislation that will undermine conservation efforts. Perhaps Trump doesn't remember that America's bald eagle population was once in big trouble and headed for possible extinction. By the efforts of many concerned people and the Endangered Species Act, eagle populations recovered and are now doing quite well. Trump is also a big supporter of the energy industry and backs the use of coal, which as a nonrenewable energy source contributes much to greenhouse gas problems.

Americans, on the other hand, care about these issues: in 2017, between 44 percent and 63 percent of the United States' population expressed concern about extinction, the loss of tropical rainforests, and pollution of air and water (including rivers and lakes), according to data gathered and reported by the National Science Foundation.

This trend is seen in other countries around the globe as well. Brazil's newest president in on track to unravel the last fifty years of environmental progress in his country, as his his administration pushes legislation that effects species, tropical forests, and indigenous people. While Madagascar's president has been in charge, a dramatic increase in illegal logging, deforestation, and biodiversity loss has occurred. At the same time China is carrying on a program of infrastructure building and support around the world that is creating havoc in natural systems. Critical habitats in the Amazon, Indonesia, and Africa are being carved up and a new dam planned in Sumatra could most likely wipe out a newly discovered species of orangutan.

Since one out of every three wildlife species in the United States is vulnerable to extinction according to the National Wildlife Federation, and since most experts agree that humans would be similarly affected by continued ecosystem degradation and loss of biodiversity, what can be done? As David Attenborough, experienced scientific videographer says, "It is that range of biodiversity that we must care for—the whole thing—rather than just one of two stars." And everyday people can help the effort! We can plant native flowers, trees, and shrubs in our yards and stop using pesticides. We can reuse, recycle, and reduce consumption. We can try to reduce energy usage and buy from local vendors. And most of all we can become educated and advocate for biodiversity and conservation efforts.

There is absolutely no doubt that the loss of biodiversity and lack of conservation efforts are a worrisome subject for humankind. The international community must do a better job of working together to slow down the rate of extinctions and degradation of natural ecosystems before it is too late. This challenging topic, its possible causes, global interest, and preventive measures are explored in diverse viewpoints from around the world in *Global Viewpoints: Biodiversity and Conservation.*

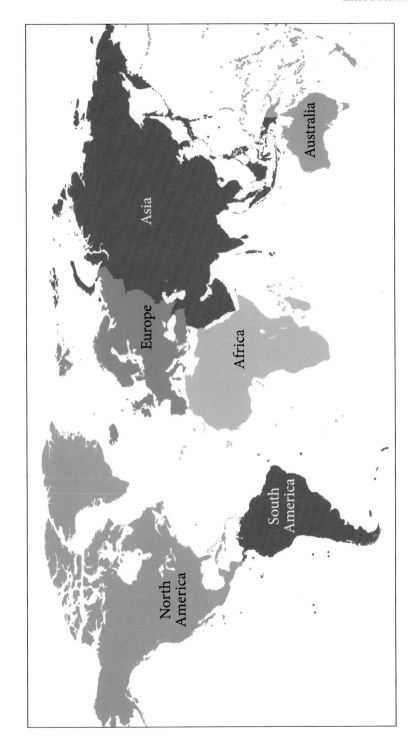

GLOBALVIEWPOINTS

CHAPTER 1

Biodiversity and Conservation Around the World

Worldwide Extinction Rates Are 1000 Times Greater Than the Natural Rate

Elizabeth Boakes and David Redding

In the following viewpoint, Elizabeth Boakes and David Redding consider the topic of extinction and whether it should matter to humans. The authors argue that the current rate of extinction is one thousand times greater than it should be according to the fossil record. Boakes and Redding examine extinction from several viewpoints, asking whether humans should be concerned, and propose that humanity should learn to control the process. Elizabeth Boakes is a teaching fellow at University College London specializing in biodiversity and ecological research. David Redding is a research fellow at the University College London.

As you read, consider the following questions:

1. As stated by the authors, what are two services provided by ecosystems?
2. What types of species are likely to become extinct according to the authors?
3. What is the counterargument against extinction as described in the viewpoint article?

"Extinction Is a Natural Process, but It's Happening at 1,000 Times the Normal Speed," by Elizabeth Boakes and David Redding, The Conversation, July 6, 2018. https://theconversation.com/extinction-is-a-natural-process-but-its-happening-at-1-000-times-the-normal-speed-99191. Licensed under CC BY-ND 4.0 International.

When Sudan the white rhino was put down by his caretakers earlier this year, it confirmed the extinction of one of the savannah's most iconic subspecies. Despite decades of effort from conservationists, including a fake Tinder profile for the animal dubbed "the most eligible bachelor in the world", Sudan proved an unwilling mate and died—the last male of his kind. His daughter and granddaughter remain—but, barring some miraculously successful IVF, it is only a matter of time.

The northern white rhino will surely be mourned, as would other stalwarts of picture books, documentaries and soft toy collections. But what about species of which of which we are less fond—or perhaps even entirely unaware? Would we grieve for obscure frogs, bothersome beetles or unsightly fungi? Extinction is, after all, inevitable in the natural world—some have even called it the "engine of evolution". So should extinction matter to us?

First of all, there are strong practical arguments against biodiversity loss. Variation, from individual genes to species, gives ecosystems resilience in the face of change. Ecosystems, in turn, hold the planet steady and provide services essential to human welfare. Forests and wetlands prevent pollutants entering our water supplies, mangroves provide coastal defence by reducing storm surges, and green spaces in urban areas lower city-dwellers' rates of mental illness. A continued loss of biodiversity will disrupt these services even further.

Seen in this light, the environmental damage caused by resource extraction and the vast changes that humans have wrought on the landscape seem extremely high risk. The world has never before experienced these disturbances all at the same time, and it is quite a gamble to assume that we can so damage our planet while at the same time maintaining the seven billion humans that live on it.

Although the unregulated plundering of the Earth's natural resources should certainly worry those brave enough to examine the evidence, it is worth specifying that extinction is an issue in its own right. Some environmental damage can be reversed, some failing ecosystems can be revived. Extinction is irrevocably final.

Uneven Losses

Studies of threatened species indicate that, by looking at their characteristics, we can predict how likely a species is to become extinct. Animals with larger bodies, for example, are more extinction-prone than those of smaller stature—and the same holds true for species at the top of the food chain. For plants, growing epiphytically (on another plant but not as a parasite) leaves them at greater risk, as does being late blooming.

This means that extinction does not occur randomly across an ecosystem, but disproportionately effects similar species that perform similar functions. Given that ecosystems rely on particular groups of organisms for particular roles, such as pollination or seed dispersal, the loss of one such group could cause considerable disruption. Imagine a disease that only killed medical professionals—it would be far more devastating for society than one which killed similar numbers of people at random.

This non-random pattern extends to the evolutionary "tree-of-life". Some closely related groups of species are restricted to the same threatened locations (such as lemurs in Madagscar) or share vulnerable characteristics (such as carnivores), meaning that the evolutionary tree could lose entire branches rather than an even scattering of leaves. Some species with few close relatives, such as the aye-aye or tuatara, are also at higher risk. Their loss would disproportionately affect the shape of the tree, not to mention erasing their weird and wonderful natural history stories.

The most regular counter argument contends that we should not worry about extinction, because it is a "natural process". First of all, so is death, but it does not follow that we meekly surrender to it (especially not prematurely or at the hands of another).

But secondly, fossil records show that current extinction levels are around 1,000 times the natural background rate. They are exacerbated by habitat loss, hunting, climate change and the introduction of invasive species and diseases. Amphibians seem particularly sensitive to environmental change, with estimated extinction rates up to 45,000 times their natural speed. Most of these extinctions are unrecorded, so we do not even know what species we are losing.

An Incalculable Cost

But does it really matter that the world contains fewer types of frog? Let's take a hypothetical small, brown African frog that becomes extinct because toxic waste pollutes its stream. The frog has never been described by science, so no one is the wiser about its loss. Putting aside disaster movie-level ecosystem collapse as a result of ongoing mass extinction, the frog's intrinsic value is a matter of opinion. It evolved over millions of years to be adapted for its particular niche—to us, the authors, the loss of that perfectly balanced individuality makes the world a lesser place.

But it is easy to moralise about biodiversity when you don't have to live alongside it. One person's marvel of nature might be another person's torment—an orangutan raiding a poor farmer's crops, or a leopard snatching a shepherd's livestock. Pathogens are also part of life's rich tapestry, but how many of us mourn the eradication of smallpox?

So how far should our aversion to extinction extend? We cannot answer this question—but like all good philosophical conundrums it belongs to everyone, to be debated in schools, cafes, bars and market places across the world. We may not all agree, but extinction is broadening its reach, so consensus and urgent action are needed if we hope to control it.

In Mozambique a Government Project Aims to Increase Biodiversity and Conservation

United Nations Development Programme

In the following viewpoint, it is stated that the United Nations Development Programme has joined with the government of Mozambique to increase the country's biodiversity and conservation. The government is aware of problems in the country that threaten endemic wildlife and attempts to curb the problems. The viewpoint analyzes the root causes of biodiversity loss and what must be done to combat the issue. UNDP Mozambique is part of the ONE UN family and works to be a key policy advisor and development partner to Mozambique.

As you read, consider the following questions:

1. According to the viewpoint, what is the aim of the Mozambique biodiversity project?
2. What are two threats to biodiversity in Mozambique according to the authors?
3. Which animal species are affected by poaching according to the viewpoint?

"Mozambique Increases Its Biodiversity Protection Efforts Through a New Project," United Nations Development Programme, May 25, 2018. Reprinted by permission.

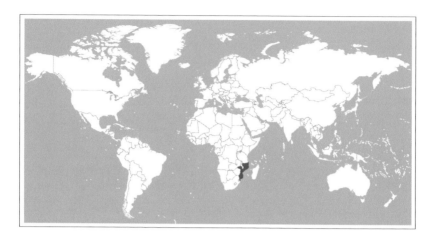

On 23 of May 2018, Mozambique Government, in partnership with the United Nations Development Program (UNDP) and the Global Environment Facility (GEF), launched a biodiversity protection project in Maputo to strengthen the conservation of endangered species in the country.

The 16.5 million project, which will be implemented until 2024 was jointly launched by the Deputy Minister for Land, the Environment and Rural Development (MITADER), Ms. Celmira Da Silva, UN Resident Coordinator and UNDP Resident Representative, Ms. Márcia de Castro and Gorongosa National Park Restoration Project Foundation Chairperson, Greg Carl.

The six-year funding is intended to strengthen the conservation of globally threatened species in Mozambique through the implementation of the Conservation Act as well as the implementation of mitigation actions against poaching in communities living in parks and buffer zones. These activities will contribute to a better use of biodiversity, as well as the expansion of conservation areas through the establishment of community conservation areas aligned with actions directed to rural development.

The Government of Mozambique is committed to the biodiversity protection agenda and has established the National Administration of Conservation Areas (ANAC) as an operational arm that ensures the integral management of the conservation areas, with the commitment to ensure that these preserve endangered species which can still be found in the country. Currently, local communities have shown a tendency to expand further into conservation areas as a result of population growth, where they seek subsistence activities that if not well managed, threaten wildlife and forestry resources leading to their unsustainable exploitation and destruction at an alarming rate, nullifying the conservation gains achieved in recent years.

According to MITADER Deputy Minister, Celmira Da Silva, one of the priority areas of government is the preservation of natural resources and environment, for a balanced and sustainable development of the national territory. Therefore, her Ministry and its partners have begun to prepare concrete actions for the protection of species threatened with extinction. "With this project, the Government of Mozambique intends to strengthen biodiversity conservation programs, with emphasis on the components to combat poaching and illegal trafficking of wildlife products," Ms. Da Silva said during the launch ceremony.

Conservation efforts have increased significantly in Mozambique since the end of the armed conflict in 1992, but there are still considerable threats affecting both terrestrial and marine biodiversity. The considerable increase in wildlife crime heightens the already existing pressures caused by uncontrolled subsistence hunting by communities living in the park and buffer zones. Since 2014, poaching has increased dramatically affecting several species including those that are in extinction, including elephants, lions, rhinos, leopards among others. The international market for wildlife products is still low risk for traffickers and is highly profitable.

As an example, the UNDP resident representative in Mozambique, Márcia Castro, revealed that more than 2,600 elephants were killed in the Niassa reserve in the period 2010-2014, which is a problem of environmental development as well as security. "So we are aware that we need to redouble our

Why You Should Care About Wildlife

Without action to protect biodiversity at a time of disappearing habitats and increased poaching, Black Rhinos, Sumatran Tigers, Western Lowland Gorillas and thousands of other animals are on the verge of extinction.

Why does that matter for people?

Biodiversity is especially important to the poor—75% of whom live in rural areas and depend on nature for their food and livelihoods. The World Bank Group is committed to protecting biodiversity around the world.

Just how important is biodiversity to those who live in extreme poverty?

Take the case of Sierra Leone, where overfishing and pollution dramatically lowered the volume and diversity of fish stocks. The Bank worked with communities to bring the marine ecosystem back to life by improving surveillance and prosecution of illegal fishing, and providing training on sustainable fishing practices. Nutrition and livelihoods have improved for local villagers as a result. "Without the fish, it would be very, very bad," says Addie, a young woman from Freetown, Sierra Leone. "For most, fish is the only protein available. Without the fish, we would get thin and weak—we would die."

The World Bank works with governments and partners around the world to protect oceans, forests, mountains, pasturelands and other ecosystems that are important for people's livelihoods.

political, institutional and financial efforts and commitments if we are to reverse the current trends in this illicit activity," she said.

Gorongosa Restoration Project Chairperson, Greg Carl believes this is yet another initiative to protect biodiversity, sensitive forest and promote income for the families living in Gorongosa. Among the actions carried out by the government and partners in favor of the maintenance of flora and fauna, stand out the approval of the law of conservation and strategy, its regulation, the action plan for the conservation of biological diversity in Mozambique.

Of the amount allocated for this project, about $ 7.5 million will support the establishment of three new community conservation areas, effectively expanding the Gorongosa National Park, as

The Bank engages communities in biodiversity conservation through incentives for nurturing the environment. In Kenya, a World Bank-supported project around Nairobi National Park paid 338 households to remove fences from their fields and allow wildlife to use an additional 22,000 hectares of adjacent land. Wildlife populations increased and families used income from this arrangement for school and medical fees, as well as livestock. The Bank also helped introduce participatory forest and pasture management in 251 communes covering 307,665 hectares in Albania. This led to sustainable management of community resources, reforestation of 1,634 hectares, and an 8% increase in incomes for participating communities.

Everything is connected. World Bank-supported reforestation in the hills of Rio, Brazil has been good for wildlife and people. "I've seen so many canaries, bluebirds, toucans and monkeys lately," said community leader Nilza Roza. Healthy wildlife populations signal that the water table, which provides reliable water for the city, is working. Reforestation has also made communities safer from landslides, restored trees that absorb carbon dioxide and earned revenue-generating carbon credits for the city.

When we protect animals and plants, we also protect the ecosystems that underlie our economies and well-being.

"Why You Should Care About Wildlife," The World Bank Group, March 3, 2014.

well as community co-management models that will be officially established in the Mecula Corridor-Marrupa in the Niassa National Reserve.

The remaining amount (equivalent to US $ 3.7 million) will support the implementation of the national strategy to combat poaching, illegal wildlife trafficking and forest crime through a coordinated approach among the various governmental entities; combating wildlife crime on the ground by strengthening enforcement operations in conservation area complexes directed as a result of joint management efforts between the ANAC and the Gorongosa Restoration Project (GRP) in Gorongosa National Park, and between ANAC and the Wildlife Conservation Society

(WCS) in the Niassa National Reserve, two national conservation areas with more than 52,000 square kilometers of surface area for the conservation of flora and fauna of international importance (equivalent to US $ 4.0 million).

There will also be support to ANAC's institutional capacity to generate knowledge in order to better capitalize on the lessons from this project (equivalent to US $ 1.2 million).

The project is anchored in the Global Wildlife Program (GWP), a Global Partnership on Wildlife Conservation and Crime Prevention for Sustainable Development through reducing poaching, reducing illicit trafficking and reducing demand.

Other initiatives include the elephant and rhino conservation action plan, which are the favorite species of poachers.

In Australia the Great Barrier Reef Is in Danger

Ove Hoegh-Guldberg and Tyrone Ridgway

In the following viewpoint, Ove Hoegh-Guldberg and Tyrone Ridgway analyze the issue of biodiversity in coral reefs. The authors use historical evidence from well-known natural historian and documentarian Sir David Attenborough. Hoegh-Guldberg and Ridgway argue that the Great Barrier Reef is suffering from climate change caused by human behaviors and maintain that steps must be taken to ensure the reef's survival. Ove Hoegh-Guldberg is a professor of marine science at the University of Queensland, Australia, and Tyrone Ridgway is a program manager at the Global Change Institute at the university.

As you read, consider the following questions:

1. What has Sir David Attenborough documented about the coral reef according to the authors?
2. What causes coral bleaching as explained by the authors?
3. According to the viewpoint, what four interventions might save the reef?

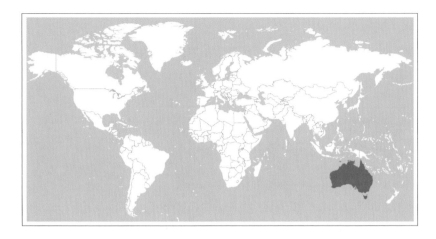

Over three weeks, Australians have been taken on an incredible journey through the biology, beauty and wonder of the Great Barrier Reef, guided by Sir David Attenborough.

As individuals who have had the privilege of working on the Reef for much of our lives, the wonderful storytelling, exquisite photography and stunning production of the Great Barrier Reef with David Attenborough has been inspiring. It's a great reminder of how lucky we are to have this wonder of nature right on our doorstep.

Particularly special has been the wonderful black-and-white footage of Sir David's first visit to the Reef in 1957, a trip down memory lane. His attachment and fascination with the Reef are hard to dismiss.

However, as the curtain closes on this wonderful series, Sir David concludes that the Reef that he visited nearly 60 years ago is very different from today.

Research backs up this personal experience. The Australian Institute of Marine Science has shown that the Great Barrier Reef has lost around 50% of its coral cover between 1985 and 2012.

A Reef in Peril

> The Great Barrier Reef is in grave danger. The twin perils brought by climate change—an increase in the temperature of the ocean and in its acidity—threaten its very existence.
>
> – Sir David Attenborough

As this television series has aired in Australia, an underwater heatwave has caused coral bleaching on 93% of the reefs that make up the Great Barrier Reef. Up to 50% of corals in the worst-affected regions may die as a result of this bleaching.

We should not be too surprised. Reef scientists have been warning about this for decades. In 1998, the warmest year on record at the time, the world lost around 16% of its coral reefs in the first global-scale mass coral bleaching event.

Before the current bleaching, the reef bleached severely in 1998 and 2002, with a substantial bleaching event in 2006 around the Keppel Islands. Outside these events, there has been moderate mass bleaching on the reef since the early 1980s (particularly 1983 and 1987), although never to the extent and intensity that we are witnessing today.

Rising Sea Temperatures

The current bleaching event has drawn widespread media coverage. One of the arguments we have seen raised is that coral bleaching is natural—and that the reef will bounce back as it always has, or even adapt to warming seas.

It is true that certain coral species, and even certain individual colonies within the same species, do perform better than others when stressed by warmer-than-normal sea temperatures. However, the extent of these differences is only 1-2°C. Given that even moderate climate change projections involve temperatures 2-3°C higher than today, these differences offer little comfort for reefs like the Great Barrier Reef in a warmer world.

The observation that corals grow in warm areas of the globe is a demonstration that corals can and do adapt to local temperatures. However, the time frames involved are hundreds of years, not a single decade. Current rates of warming are much faster than anything for tens of millions of years, which makes the prospect of evolution keeping pace with a changing ocean even more improbable.

Mass bleaching is a new phenomenon that was first reported in the early 1980s. Before this, there are no reports of corals bleaching en masse across any coral reef or ocean region.

Experts are in agreement that mass coral bleaching and death on the Great Barrier Reef is driven by climate change resulting from human activities (mainly burning fossil fuels). This is the conclusion at the heart of the latest consensus of the United Nations scientific report.

Rising sea temperatures coupled with strong El Niños are unfortunately pushing corals to their thermal tolerance limits and beyond. It only takes a temperature increase of 1-2°C to disrupt the special relationship between corals and tiny marine algae that live inside their tissue, resulting in bleached corals.

In fact, as CO_2 concentrations rise, sea temperatures will continue to climb—increasing the likelihood that mass coral bleaching events will become more frequent and more destructive. Recent research has shown that near-future increases in local temperature of as little as 0.5°C may lead to significant degradation of the Great Barrier Reef.

Rising temperatures are not the only climate threat. Cyclones are predicted to become stronger (if less frequent) in a warmer world. Since 2005 there have been eight cyclones on the reef of category 3 or above—more than previous decades. We would argue this is evidence that these predictions are already coming true and form part of our current reality.

Heat stress is not just affecting corals on the Great Barrier Reef either. We are seeing reports of bleaching across all of Australia's coral real estate (Coral Sea, Torres Strait, Kimberley, North West Shelf), the South Pacific and the central and western Indian Ocean.

Panda Conservation

The good news is that giant panda numbers are increasing. Slowly but surely this remarkable species is edging away from the brink of extinction—thanks to a host of successful conservation projects.

But pandas still face a number of threats, particularly habitat loss and fragmentation, so extra efforts are needed to ensure that they continue to survive and thrive.

Creating new reserves and linking up existing panda populations are key to the species' future. The Chinese authorities have increased the number of panda reserves to 67 in recent years, but this still leaves around 1/3rd of wild pandas outside protected areas.

The Chinese government, in partnership with WWF, has also developed bamboo corridors to link pockets of forest, allowing the pandas within them to move to new areas, find more food and meet more potential breeding mates.

But with panda habitat continuing to be fragmented by roads, railways and other human development, additional corridors will be needed to connect isolated panda populations.

The success of panda conservation in recent years owes much to the dedication and determination of Chinese and international researchers working with the governments, universities and conservations organisations, such as WWF.

By spending countless hours monitoring and researching, they have been able to develop an accurate picture of the panda's population status and current threats, and formulate effective measures that have reversed the panda's decline.

Ongoing research and monitoring of pandas and their fragile habitat will be vital to ensuring that the conservation successes of the past few decades are not undermined. And that giant panda numbers continue to recover.

Camera traps are a critical research tool because of the difficulty of locating pandas in their remote, mountain habitat.

The cameras are triggered by movement and, along with GPS technology, are helping to create a more accurate picture of the number of pandas in the wild.

It is likely only a matter of time before we start to see reports of bleaching from other coral reefs around the world. We are indeed dealing with changing times and a global issue.

It's Not Too Late to Act

It's not too late to act—but we will need very deep and significant action to occur within three to five years or face a collapse of ecosystems like the Great Barrier Reef.

Climate change is just one of the threats facing the Great Barrier Reef. Fortunately, it is not too late to give the reef a fighting chance.

However, it does require strong, immediate and decisive action from our political leaders.

In the lead-up to the federal election, we believe that four major steps are required by our leaders to ensure a future for the Reef:

1. Mitigate: we need to—as per the Paris Agreement—keep average global surface temperature increases to below 2.0°C, and hopefully 1.5°C in the long term. This means we must adopt a pathway that will bring our greenhouse gas emissions to zero over the next few decades. Our leaders must live up to the global agreement that they committed to in Paris at COP21.

2. Invest: we need to ultimately close our coal mines and stop searching for more fossil fuels. The experts tell us that we must leave 80% of known fossil fuels in the ground. Let's invest in coral, renewables and the planet, and not in coal, emissions and ecosystem collapse.

3. Strengthen: we need an urgent and concerted effort to reduce other non-climate change threats to build the resilience of the reef so it can better withstand the impacts of climate change over the coming years.

4. Integrate: Australian and Queensland governments have begun a process to address declining reef health through the Reef 2050 Long-term Sustainability Plan. This plan has a strong focus on coastal water quality. The 2050 Reef Plan

and its resourcing will need to consider climate change—especially given that it is likely to make achieving the objectives of the plan even more challenging and impossible (if no action). Otherwise we run the risk of ending up with a great plan for improving water quality by 2050 but no Great Barrier Reef.

We hope that Sir David Attenborough will help inspire Australians to demand action from their political leaders to ensure that this natural wonder of the world continues to inspire, employ, educate and generate income for generations to come.

It seems fitting to end with Sir David's closing words with a call to our political leaders and fellow Australians:

Do we really care so little about the earth upon which we live that we don't wish to protect one of its greatest wonders from the consequences of our behaviours?

After all, it is our Great Barrier Reef—let's keep it great. Or at least let's fight to keep it.

In Ecuador the Government Acts to Save Galapagos Sharks

Shelia Hu and Michelle Bender

In the following viewpoint Shelia Hu and Michelle Bender analyze the actions of the Ecuadorian government aimed at preserving shark species that populate the Galapagos Islands. The authors maintain that the areas protected by Ecuadorian law will also serve to protect other marine species besides the sharks. Additionally, the authors report on the idea that people will need to be educated and buy into the program. Shelia Hu and Michelle Bender write for the Earth Law Center, a nonprofit organization that works to transform laws to support the rights of nature.

As you read, consider the following questions:

1. What are three marine species that live in the Galapagos Marine Reserve as stated by the viewpoint?
2. What is a "no-take" zone as explained by the authors?
3. What secondary projects listed in the viewpoint could help serve Galapagos conservation efforts?

"Rights of Nature to Save the Endangered Sharks of the Galapagos," by Shelia Hu and Michelle Bender, Earth Law Center, July 9, 2018. Reprinted by permission.

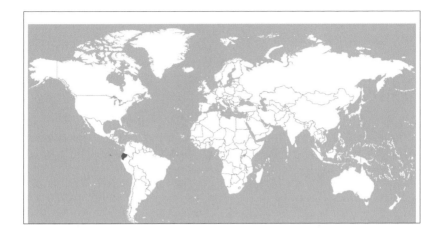

With 34 of the globe's 440 known species, the Galapagos Islands have the highest abundance of sharks in the world.[1]

A UNESCO World Heritage center, the Galapagos lies about 1,000 kilometers from the Ecuadorian Coast. Three major tectonic plates—Nazca, Cocos and Pacific—meet here. The ongoing seismic and volcanic activity create a truly unique ecosystem. The Galapagos achieved fame in scientific circles when Charles Darwin published the "Voyage of the Beagle" in 1839.[2]

The Galápagos Marine Reserve is one of the largest marine reserves in the world, covering a total area of 130,000 square kilometers of Pacific Ocean and featuring a dynamic mix of tropical and Antarctic currents and rich areas of upwelling water.

Consequently, the Galapagos Marine Reserve (GMR) contains an extraordinary range of biological communities, hosting such diverse organisms as penguins, fur seals, tropical corals, and large schools of hammerhead sharks. The GMR has a high proportion of endemic marine species—between 10% and 30% in most taxonomic groups—and supports the coastal wildlife of the terrestrial Galapagos National Park (GNP). It also appears to play an important role in the migratory routes of pelagic organisms such as marine turtles, cetaceans and the world's largest fish, the whale shark (Rhincodon typus).[3]

In 2016, the President of Ecuador, Rafael Correa, announced the creation of a new marine sanctuary to protect the water around the Galapagos Islands. The sanctuary is designed to fall around the islands of Darwin and Wolf in order to protect the world's greatest concentration of sharks.[4]

The area will include 39,000 square kilometers within the Galapagos Marine Reserve, an area in which industrial fishing has been banned since 1998 but where smaller fishing operations are allowed.[5] The new shark sanctuary will mean several areas within the GMR will be designated as "no-take" zones where no fishing of any kind will be allowed. The sanctuary will protect around 32% of waters surrounding the Galapagos, with no fishing activity, mining, or oil drilling allowed at all.[6]

The extra step of protection is needed as the ecosystem faces the increased stressors of climate change, industrial trawlers, and illegal fishing.

The Mystery of the Pregnant Whale Sharks

The largest fish in the ocean, the whale shark eats plankton and other small fish—collected as the whale shark swims. Preferring warm waters, whale sharks populate all tropical seas. They are known to migrate every spring to the continental shelf of the central west coast of Australia. The coral spawning of the area's Ningaloo Reef provides the whale shark with an abundant supply of plankton.[7]

There isn't much else known about this type of shark and its social habits. They haven't been studied as well as other sea creatures, according to the IUCN.[8]

The whale sharks in the Galapagos Marine Reserve, unlike elsewhere, tend to be large mature females (99.8%), and over 90% appear to be pregnant.[9] To find out more about why these pregnant whales stopover at the Galapagos (but with no sign of newborns), the Galapagos Whale Shark Project launched. After tracking it was found that Darwin island provides an important point for navigation for the sharks, on their way to feeding grounds in the Pacific Ocean.[10]

Hammerhead Nursery Found in Galapagos Waters

A nursery for scalloped hammerhead sharks was recently discovered along the coast of the Santa Cruz Island in the Galapagos, good news for better understanding and protecting an endangered species.[11]

Their wide-set eyes give them a better visual range than most other sharks. And by spreading their highly specialized sensory organs over their wide, mallet-shaped heads, they can more thoroughly scan the ocean for food. One group of sensory organs is the ampullae of Lorenzini. It allows sharks to detect, among other things, the electrical fields created by prey animals. The hammerheads' increased ampullae sensitivity allows them to find their favorite meal, stingrays, which usually bury themselves under the sand.[12]

After a nine to ten month gestation, scalloped hammerhead sharks give birth to their pups who can then slowly mature into adulthood in the well-protected, food-rich environment safe from many of their natural predators (like other sharks) in the open ocean.[13]

Threats Facing Sharks in Galapagos Waters

Sharks are under serious threat around the globe. It is estimated that up to 70 million sharks are killed by people every year, due to both commercial and recreational fishing. The International Union for Conservation of Nature (IUCN) has classified 64 of the 440 shark species as endangered, and one-third at risk of extinction, according to its "Red List" criteria.[14] Sharks are caught intentionally or as accidental "by-catch" in virtually all types of fisheries worldwide.[15]

Most sharks are long-living species that grow slowly, mature late, and have low reproduction rates. These biological factors make sharks particularly vulnerable to overfishing and mean that populations can be slow to recover once depleted. The continuous depletion and even eradication of these top predators in the structure of many marine habitats will have catastrophic consequences for ecosystems such as coral reefs and may cause the extinction of many other interdependent species.[16]

While sharks in Galapagos are protected by the Galapagos Marine Reserve, they roam quite far and can be affected by illegal fishing and bycatch in fisheries targeted at other species.[17]

Over 6,600 dead sharks, mostly hammerheads but also silky, thresher and mako sharks—which are off-limits to industrial fishers within the marine reserve—were found on an unauthorized ship in the Galapagos Reserve in August 2017. An Ecuadorean judge has since convicted the ship's 20 crew members of possessing and transporting protected species. In addition to prison sentences, the ruling also fined them $5.9 million.

"The sentence marks a milestone in regional environmental law and an opportunity to survive for migratory species," the country's Ministry of Environment said in a statement. This case also marked the first conviction of an environmental crime in 14 years of Galapagos law and set a precedent for prosecuting shark finning and other crimes against nature in the Galapagos (Franco Fernando, 2015).

Ecuador, a World Leader in Rights of Nature

In 2008, Ecuador became the first country to adopt Rights of Nature into its Constitution. The Constitution, endows "Nature or Pachamama, where life is reproduced and exists" with inalienable rights to "exist, persist, maintain and regenerate its vital cycles, structure, functions and its processes in evolution."

The Constitution also gives nature the right to restoration and the people the right to "live in a healthy and ecologically balanced environment that guarantees sustainability and the good way of living." It is the responsibility of the Ecuadorian State to "respect the rights of nature, preserve a healthy environment and use natural resources rationally, sustainably and durably" and to provide incentives to the citizens to "protect nature and to promote respect for all the elements comprising an ecosystem."[18]

Ocean Rights Can Help the Sharks of the Galapagos

Earth Law Center is working with partners in Ecuador including Coordinadora de Organizaciones para la Defensa de la Naturaleza y el Ambiente (CEDENMA), the Global Alliance for the Rights of Nature (GARN) and Hugo Echeverria to ensure the constitutional amendment is implemented with respect to ocean governance.

Implementing ocean rights and expanding protection of the Galapagos, will also help Ecuador achieve its goals within the Convention on Biological Diversity (CBD) and United Nations Sustainable Development goals; including expanding marine protected areas to 8170 square kilometers.[19]

The Marine Reserve represents one of the first applications of Rights of Nature to ocean protection internationally. The Special Law of the Galapagos's guiding principle for governance is "An equilibrium among the society, the economy, and nature; cautionary measures to limit risks; respect for the rights of nature; restoration in cases of damage; and citizen participation." Due to this principle, the Galapagos Marine Reserve and human activity within is held to fairly high standards.

However, more must be done to proactively protect sharks within and surrounding the Reserve.

To date, the judicial system has led the way on implementing rights of nature in Ecuador. These cases are one way to establish the standards for Rights of Nature. In other words, these cases help define what rights nature means, what rights nature has, and at what level we decide nature's rights are being violated. Similar to countries where common law plays a role in creating the norms of society. The courts can create the rules and norms for rights of nature that society should adhere to going forward.

The Giant Panda

The giant panda is perhaps the most powerful symbol in the world when it comes to species conservation. For WWF, panda has a special significance since it has been the organization's symbol since 1961 when WWF was formed. In China, it is a national treasure. It's also the first species that WWF protected in China when being invited by Chinese government to work in China.

There are 3 million ha of giant panda habitat among 5 isolated mountain pitches in China. A 2004 survey found that there are 1600 giant pandas in the wild, yet they are fragmented to more than 18 small populations. Together with Chinese government, WWF China has been promoting a giant panda protection network. So far, the network has already included 62 nature reserves, and a couple of forest farms, migration corridors, and sustainably managed forests. It also covers 57 per cent of giant panda habitat and 71 per cent of its population in the wild.

WWF China's Work to Support Panda Protection:

- Giant Panda Conservation Network for 3 Million Hectares of Habitat
- Giant Panda Friendly Sustainable Forest Management for 7 Critical Forests

Additionally, despite the uniqueness and fragility of the Islands, some do not see themselves as living within a National Park. According to Arturo Izurieta, Director of the Charles Darwin Foundation, policy decisions need to be made as if we [the people] live within a National Park. To do so, a behavioral shift is needed in those living on the island, and rights of nature concepts need to be inserted within the education system.

The Galapagos shows how essential it is to have local community support for conservation. For example, when the President proposed the Shark Sanctuary in 2016, there was pushback from local fishermen because the Sanctuary was created top-down with encouragement from the international community. Though they do not fish shark, their artisanal fishing grounds are within the proposed area. The Sanctuary has since been postponed.

- Community Co-management Forests
- High Conservation Value Forest
- Payment for Ecological Services
- Models for Sustainable Livelihoods
- Capacity Building on Alternative Livelihoods and Energy
- Community Revolving Fund Initiative
- Sustainable Management of Non-Timber Forest Products and Plants used in Traditional Chinese Medicine
- Green Product Certification and Marketing
- Eco-tourism
- Capacity Building for NGOs
- Human-wildlife Conflict Management

In the long run, WWF has a vision that by 2030, a viable giant panda population will live in the well-managed forests of the upper reaches of the Yangtze River, which in turn will provide ecological services to the people living further downstream.

"Giant Panda," WWF - World Wide Fund For Nature. https://en.wwfchina.org/en/ what_we_do/species/fs/panda/. Licensed Under CC BY-NC 4.0 International.

What Are Some Pathways for Proactive Shark Conservation?

One way to implement the rights of nature in the Galapagos, is to pass a decree declaring the Reserve (and proposed Sanctuary) as a legal entity, subject to basic rights. Defining in law the Reserve as a legal entity recognizes the area as a living whole, and legally requires that the State protects the rights of the ecosystem and species within.

Similarly the management plan could explicitly define the highest objective for management as conserving the Reserve in as close to its natural state as possible. Protecting and restoring the ecosystem for its own benefit can occur only if conservation objectives are prioritized over human-centered objectives, such as economic development. Secondary objectives can include tourism, fisheries, recreation, education and scientific research, but these must also be explicitly defined as secondary objectives. Such an approach has already been implemented in the Marae Moana of the Cook Islands, and is proving successful.

In countries, such as New Zealand, guardians are being appointed on the management boards for the protected area that represent the ecosystem's interests and ensures it's rights are not being violated; they will review decisions, monitor compliance and develop new rules to protect the Reserve. Such an approach can also work in Ecuador, allowing the guardians to not only be the voice for sharks and the Reserve in decisionmaking but to use their standing to bring legal action upon parties involved with activities directly affecting the health and well-being of sharks and the Reserve.

Finally, management could fully take into account all species interactions and land-based activities. In order to manage human activity holistically within the Reserve, criteria for decisionmaking can be further developed in line with Rights of Nature to ensure activities respect the rights of nature. Such criteria can include:

- Reflecting on the true cost of our activities, externalities and their impacts, which includes costs to the marine ecosystem and its ability to renew and restore itself.

- Evaluate decisions using attributes and scores that assign the highest scores to those activities and regulations that lead to the fulfillment of the conservation objectives.

- Application of the Precautionary Principle which puts the burden of proof on those wishing to take potentially harmful action—to prevent harm before it occurs.

- Development of alternative livelihoods that allow for both human and ecological interests to thrive.

- Impacts to keystone species, such as sharks, are given priority in decisionmaking.

The Earth Law Framework for Marine Protected Areas further outlines how rights of nature can be implemented in the Galapagos Marine Reserve. Employing this framework will help Ecuador implement rights of nature throughout their oceanscape.

More about Coordinadora de Organizaciones para la Defensa de la Naturaleza y el Ambiente (CEDENMA) based in Ecuador with the purpose of politically representing the expression or collective opinion of the group of Ecuadorian organizations and networks dedicated to the conservation of Nature and the environment, the projection of the environmental dimension and, the promotion and achievement of the respectful and sustainable use of natural assets. https://www.cedenma.org/

Notes

[1] https://galapagosconservation.org.uk/sharks-galapagos-islands/; https://www.theguardian.com/environment/2016/mar/21/ecuador-creates-galapagos-marine-sanctuary-to-protect-sharks

[2] https://whc.unesco.org/en/list/1

[3] https://www.galapagoswhaleshark.org/the-project/why-study-whale-sharks/

[4] "Ecuador creates new marine sanctuary to protect sharks", 21 March 2016, Galapagos Conservancy, https://www.galapagos.org/newsroom/new-marine-sanctuary/ Accessed: 7 June 2018

[5] "Ecuador creates new marine sanctuary to protect sharks", 21 March 2016, Galapagos Conservancy, https://www.galapagos.org/newsroom/new-marine-sanctuary/ Accessed: 7 June 2018

[6] Ibid.

[7] https://www.nationalgeographic.com/animals/fish/w/whale-shark/

[8] https://www.livescience.com/55412-whale-sharks.html

[9] https://galapagosconservation.org.uk/projects/whale-shark-monitoring/

[10] https://www.galapagoswhaleshark.org/the-project/what-we-discovered-so-far/

[11] https://news.nationalgeographic.com/2018/01/hammerhead-shark-nursery-discovery-galapagos-spd/

[12] https://www.nationalgeographic.com/animals/fish/group/hammerhead-sharks/

[13] https://news.nationalgeographic.com/2018/01/hammerhead-shark-nursery-discovery-galapagos-spd/

[14] https://www.theguardian.com/science/2009/jun/25/sharks-extinction-iucn-red-list

[15] http://sharksmou.org/threats-to-sharks

[16] http://sharksmou.org/threats-to-sharks

[17] https://galapagosconservation.org.uk/sharks-galapagos-islands/

[18] Republic of Ecuador, Constitution of 2008, available at: http://pdba.georgetown.edu/Constitutions/Ecuador/englis h08.html.

[19] Ibid.

The World's Biodiversity Needs to Be Rescued

Damian Carrington

In the following viewpoint Damian Carrington outlines the argument accepted by many experts—that loss of biodiversity is an urgent threat to us all. Carrington argues that species have already become extinct, and that the process of extinction, which has accelerated beyond natural rates, is going to change the world's biodiversity and severely affect humans. In the end, Carrington offers several suggestions that may help the problem. Damian Carrington is the environmental editor for The Guardian.

As you read, consider the following questions:

1. What is the highest level of biodiversity as explained by the viewpoint?
2. How does biodiversity benefit humanity according to Carrington?
3. According to the author, what is the ultimate threat to humanity?

"What Is Biodiversity and Why Does It Matter to Us?" by Damian Carrington, Guardian News & Media Limited, March 12, 2018. Reprinted by permission.

B iodiversity is the variety of life on Earth, in all its forms and all its interactions. If that sounds bewilderingly broad, that's because it is. Biodiversity is the most complex feature of our planet and it is the most vital. "Without biodiversity, there is no future for humanity," says Prof David Macdonald, at Oxford University.

The term was coined in 1985—a contraction of "biological diversity"—but the huge global biodiversity losses now becoming apparent represent a crisis equalling—or quite possibly surpassing—climate change.

More formally, biodiversity is comprised of several levels, starting with genes, then individual species, then communities of creatures and finally entire ecosystems, such as forests or coral reefs, where life interplays with the physical environment. These myriad interactions have made Earth habitable for billions of years.

A more philosophical way of viewing biodiversity is this: it represents the knowledge learned by evolving species over millions of years about how to survive through the vastly varying environmental conditions Earth has experienced. Seen like that, experts warn, humanity is currently "burning the library of life".

Do Animals and Bugs Really Matter to Me?

For many people living in towns and cities, wildlife is often something you watch on television. But the reality is that the air you breathe, the water you drink and the food you eat all ultimately rely on biodiversity. Some examples are obvious: without plants there would be no oxygen and without bees to pollinate there would be no fruit or nuts.

Others are less obvious—coral reefs and mangrove swamps provide invaluable protection from cyclones and tsunamis for those living on coasts, while trees can absorb air pollution in urban areas.

Others appear bizarre—tropical tortoises and spider monkeys seemingly have little to do with maintaining a stable climate. But the dense, hardwood trees that are most effective in removing carbon dioxide from the atmosphere rely on their seeds being dispersed by these large fruit-eaters.

When scientists explore each ecosystem, they find countless such interactions, all honed by millions of years of evolution. If undamaged, this produces a finely balanced, healthy system which contributes to a healthy sustainable planet.

The sheer richness of biodiversity also has human benefits. Many new medicines are harvested from nature, such as a fungi that grows on the fur of sloths and can fight cancer. Wild varieties of domesticated animals and crops are also crucial as some will have already solved the challenge of, for example, coping with drought or salty soils.

If money is a measure, the services provided by ecosystems are estimated to be worth trillions of dollars—double the world's GDP. Biodiversity loss in Europe alone costs the continent about 3% of its GDP, or €450m (£400m), a year.

From an aesthetic point of view, every one of the millions of species is unique, a natural work of art that cannot be recreated once lost. "Each higher organism is richer in information than a Caravaggio painting, a Bach fugue, or any other great work," wrote Prof Edward O Wilson, often called the "father of biodiversity", in a seminal paper in 1985.

Just How Diverse Is Biodiversity?

Mind-bogglingly diverse. The simplest aspect to consider is species. About 1.7 million species of animals, plants and fungi have been recorded, but there are likely to be 8-9 million and possibly up to 100 million. The heartland of biodiversity is the tropics, which teems with species. In 15 hectares (37 acres) of Borneo forest, for example, there are 700 species of tree—the same number as the whole of North America.

Recent work considering diversity at a genetic level has suggested that creatures thought to be a single species could in some cases actually be dozens. Then add in bacteria and viruses, and the number of distinct organisms may well be in the billions. A single spoonful of soil—which ultimately provides 90% of all food—contains 10,000 to 50,000 different types of bacteria.

The concern is that many species are being lost before we are even aware of them, or the role they play in the circle of life.

How Bad Is It?

Very. The best studied creatures are the ones like us—large mammals. Tiger numbers, for example, have plunged by 97% in the last century. In many places, bigger animals have already been wiped out by humans—think dodos or woolly mammoths.

The extinction rate of species is now thought to be about 1,000 times higher than before humans dominated the planet, which may be even faster than the losses after a giant meteorite wiped out the dinosaurs 65m years ago. The sixth mass extinction in geological history has already begun, according to some scientists.

Lack of data means the "red list", produced by the International Union for Conservation of Nature, has only assessed 5% of known species. But for the best known groups it finds many are threatened: 25% of mammals, 41% of amphibians and 13% of birds.

Species extinction provides a clear but narrow window on the destruction of biodiversity—it is the disappearance of the last member of a group that is by definition rare. But new studies are examining the drop in the total number of animals, capturing the plight of the world's most common creatures.

The results are scary. Billions of individual populations have been lost all over the planet, with the number of animals living on Earth having plunged by half since 1970. Abandoning the normally sober tone of scientific papers, researchers call the massive loss of wildlife a "biological annihilation" representing a "frightening assault on the foundations of human civilisation".

What About Under the Sea?

Humans may lack gills but that has not protected marine life. The situation is no better—and perhaps even less understood—in the two-thirds of the planet covered by oceans. Seafood is the critical source of protein for more than 2.5 billion people but rampant overfishing has caused catches to fall steadily since their peak in 1996 and now more than half the ocean is industrially fished.

What About Bugs—Don't Cockroaches Survive Anything?

More than 95% of known species lack a backbone—there are about as many species in the staphylinidae family of beetles alone as there are total vertebrates, such as mammals, fish and birds. Altogether, there are at least a million species of insect and another 300,000 spiders, molluscs and crustaceans.

But the recent revelation that 75% of flying insects were lost in the last 25 years in Germany—and likely elsewhere—indicates the massacre of biodiversity is not sparing creepy crawlies. And insects really matter, not just as pollinators but as predators of pests, decomposers of waste and, crucially, as the base of the many wild food chains that support ecosystems.

"If we lose the insects then everything is going to collapse," says Prof Dave Goulson of Sussex University, UK. "We are currently on course for ecological Armageddon."

Even much-loathed parasites are important. One-third could be wiped out by climate change, making them among the most threatened groups on Earth. But scientists warn this could destabilise ecosystems, unleashing unpredictable invasions of surviving parasites into new areas.

What's Destroying Biodiversity?

We are, particularly as the human population rises and wild areas are razed to create farmland, housing and industrial sites. The felling of forests is often the first step and 30m hectares—the area of the Britain and Ireland—were lost globally in 2016.

Poaching and unsustainable hunting for food is another major factor. More than 300 mammal species, from chimpanzees to hippos to bats, are being eaten into extinction.

Pollution is a killer too, with orcas and dolphins being seriously harmed by long-lived industrial pollutants. Global trade contributes further harm: amphibians have suffered one of the greatest declines of all animals due to a fungal disease thought to be spread around the world by the pet trade. Global shipping has also spread highly damaging invasive species around the planet, particularly rats.

The hardest hit of all habitats may be rivers and lakes, with freshwater animal populations in these collapsing by 81% since 1970, following huge water extraction for farms and people, plus pollution and dams.

Could the Loss of Biodiversity Be a Greater Threat to Humanity Than Climate Change?

Yes—nothing on Earth is experiencing more dramatic change at the hands of human activity. Changes to the climate are reversible, even if that takes centuries or millennia. But once species become extinct, particularly those unknown to science, there's no going back.

At the moment, we don't know how much biodiversity the planet can lose without prompting widespread ecological collapse. But one approach has assessed so-called "planetary boundaries", thresholds in Earth systems that define a "safe operating space for humanity". Of the nine considered, just biodiversity loss and nitrogen pollution are estimated to have been crossed, unlike CO_2 levels, freshwater used and ozone losses.

What Can Be Done?

Giving nature the space and protection it needs is the only answer. Wildlife reserves are the obvious solution, and the world currently protects 15% of land and 7% of the oceans. But some argue that half the land surface must be set aside for nature.

However, the human population is rising and wildlife reserves don't work if they hinder local people making a living. The poaching crisis for elephants and rhinos in Africa is an extreme example. Making the animals worth more alive than dead is the key, for example by supporting tourism or compensating farmers for livestock killed by wild predators.

But it can lead to tough choices. "Trophy hunting" for big game is anathema for many. But if the shoots are done sustainably—only killing old lions, for example—and the money raised protects a large swath of land, should it be permitted?

We can all help. Most wildlife is destroyed by land being cleared for cattle, soy, palm oil, timber and leather. Most of us consume these products every day, with palm oil being found in many foods and toiletries. Choosing only sustainable options helps, as does eating less meat, particularly beef, which has an outsized environmental hoofprint.

Another approach is to highlight the value of biodiversity by estimating the financial value of the ecosystem services provided as "natural capital". Sometimes this can lead to real savings. Over the last 20 years, New York has spent $2bn protecting the natural watershed that supplies the city with clean water. It has worked so well that 90% of the water needs no further filtering: building a water treatment plant instead would have cost $10bn.

What's Next?

Locating the tipping point that moves biodiversity loss into ecological collapse is an urgent priority. Biodiversity is vast and research funds are small, but speeding up analysis might help, from automatically identifying creatures using machine learning to real-time DNA sequencing.

There is even an initiative that aims to create an open-source genetic database for all plants, animals and single-cell organisms on the planet. It argues that by creating commercial opportunities—such as self-driving car algorithms inspired by Amazonian ants—it could provide the incentive to preserve Earth's biodiversity.

However, some researchers say the dire state of biodiversity is already clear enough and that the missing ingredient is political will.

A global treaty, the Convention on Biological Diversity (CBD), has set many targets. Some are likely to be reached, for example protecting 17% of all land and 10% of the oceans by 2020. Others, such as making all fishing sustainable by the same date are not.

The 196 nations that are members of the CBD next meet in Egypt in November.

In his 1985 text, Prof E O Wilson, concluded: "This being the only living world we are ever likely to know, let us join to make the most of it." That call is more urgent than ever.

Periodical and Internet Sources Bibliography

The following articles have been selected to supplement the diverse views presented in this chapter.

David Beard, "Scientists Just Made a Remarkable Discovery in the Galápagos Islands," *Mother Jones*, February 27, 2019, https://www.motherjones.com/media/2019/02/recharge-43-fernandina-giant-tortoise/

Andy Coghlan, "Europe is Rapidly Losing Its Biodiversity and Wildlife Habitats," *New Scientist*, May 18, 2015, https://www.newscientist.com/article/dn27543-europe-is-rapidly-losing-its-biodiversity-and-wildlife-habitats/

Natasha Daly, "How the Oceans Have Become Hostile for Animals," *National Geographic*, April 4, 2019, https://www.nationalgeographic.com/animals/2019/04/extreme-animals-live-in-oceans/

Russell Mclendon, "5 Reasons Why Biodiversity Is a Big Deal, Mother Nature Network, May 6, 2019, https://www.mnn.com/earth-matters/wilderness-resources/blogs/why-biodiversity-big-deal

Noel D. Preece, "Australia Among the World's Worst on Biodiversity Conservation," The Conversation, November 20, 2017, https://theconversation.com/australia-among-the-worlds-worst-on-biodiversity-conservation-86685

Lauryn Stalter, "Diversity Is Key to a Resilient Future Forest," Parks & Recreation, April 5, 2019, https://www.nrpa.org/parks-recreation-magazine/2019/april/diversity-is-key-to-a-resilient-future-forest/

Luke Taylor, "The Forgotten Riches of the Most Densely Biodiverse Country on Earth," *New Scientist*, April 10, 2019, https://www.newscientist.com/article/mg24232250-400-the-forgotten-riches-of-the-most-densely-biodiverse-country-on-earth/

Jonathan Watts, "China Urged to Lead Way in Efforts to Save Life on Earth," *Guardian*, November 29, 2018, https://www.theguardian.com/environment/2018/nov/29/china-urged-lead-way-efforts-save-life-on-earth-un

GLOBAL VIEWPOINTS

 CHAPTER 2

What Causes the Loss of Biodiversity?

Human Population Growth Is Causing Problems Worldwide

Center for Biological Diversity

In the following viewpoint, authors at the Center for Biological Diversity maintain that human population growth has caused the extinction of animals in the past and will continue to do so in the future. The authors argue that several factors demonstrate that humans will continue to dominate over the planet in many ways, all of which are because of unsustainable human populations. The Center for Biological Diversity believes that humans are deeply linked to nature, a world with diverse wild animals and plants.

As you read, consider the following questions:

1. How long ago did humans migrate into North America according to the authors?
2. What caused the third wave of extinctions as stated by the viewpoint?
3. What percentage of land on Earth is devoted to food production according to the viewpoint?

W e're in the midst of the Earth's sixth mass extinction crisis. Harvard biologist E. O. Wilson estimates that 30,000 species per year (or three species per hour) are being driven to extinction. Compare this to the natural background rate of one extinction per million species per year, and you can see why scientists refer to it as a crisis unparalleled in human history.

The current mass extinction differs from all others in being driven by a single species rather than a planetary or galactic physical process. When the human race—Homo sapiens sapiens—migrated out of Africa to the Middle East 90,000 years ago, to Europe and Australia 40,000 years ago, to North America 12,500 years ago, and to the Caribbean 8,000 years ago, waves of extinction soon followed. The colonization-followed-by-extinction pattern can be seen as recently as 2,000 years ago, when humans colonized Madagascar and quickly drove elephant birds, hippos, and large lemurs extinct.[1]

The first wave of extinctions targeted large vertebrates hunted by hunter-gatherers. The second, larger wave began 10,000 years ago as the discovery of agriculture caused a population boom and a need to plow wildlife habitats, divert streams, and maintain large herds of domestic cattle. The third and largest wave began in 1800 with the harnessing of fossil fuels. With enormous, cheap energy at its disposal, the human population grew rapidly from 1 billion in 1800 to 2 billion in 1930, 4 billion in 1975, and over 7.5 billion today. If the current course is not altered, we'll reach 8 billion by 2020 and 9 to 15 billion (likely the former) by 2050. No population of a large vertebrate animal in the history of the planet has grown that much, that fast, or with such devastating consequences to its fellow earthlings. Humans' impact has been so profound that scientists have proposed that the Holocene era be declared over and the current epoch (beginning in about 1900) be called the Anthropocene: the age when the "global environmental effects of increased human population and economic development" dominate planetary physical, chemical, and biological conditions.[2]

- Humans annually absorb 42 percent of the Earth's terrestrial net primary productivity,30 percent of its marine net primary productivity, and 50 percent of its fresh water.[3]

- Forty percent of the planet's land is devoted to human food production, up from 7 percent in 1700.[3]

- Fifty percent of the planet's land mass has been transformed for human use.[3]

- More atmospheric nitrogen is now fixed by humans that all other natural processes combined.[3]

The authors of Human Domination of Earth's Ecosystems, including the current director of the National Oceanic and Atmospheric Administration, concluded:

> [A]ll of these seemingly disparate phenomena trace to a single cause: the growing scale of the human enterprise. The rates, scales, kinds, and combinations of changes occurring now are fundamentally different from those at any other time in history. … We live on a human-dominated planet and the momentum of human population growth, together with the imperative for further economic development in most of the world, ensures that our dominance will increase.

Predicting local extinction rates is complex due to differences in biological diversity, species distribution, climate, vegetation, habitat threats, invasive species, consumption patterns, and enacted conservation measures. One constant, however, is human population pressure. A study of 114 nations found that human population density predicted with 88-percent accuracy the number of endangered birds and mammals as identified by the International Union for the Conservation of Nature.[4] Current population growth trends indicate that the number of threatened species will increase by 7 percent over the next 20 years and 14 percent by 2050. And that's without the addition of global warming impacts.

When the population of a species grows beyond the capacity of its environment to sustain it, it reduces that capacity below the original level, ensuring an eventual population crash.

"The density of people is a key factor in species threats," said Jeffrey McKee, one of the study's authors. "If other species follow the same pattern as the mammals and birds ... we are facing a serious threat to global biodiversity associated with our growing human population."[5]

So where does wildlife stand today in relation to 7.5 billion people? Worldwide, 12 percent of mammals, 12 percent of birds, 31 percent of reptiles, 30 percent of amphibians, and 37 percent of fish are threatened with extinction.[6] Not enough plants and invertebrates have been assessed to determine their global threat level, but it is severe.

Extinction is the most serious, utterly irreversible effect of unsustainable human population. But unfortunately, many analyses of what a sustainable human population level would look like presume that the goal is simply to keep the human race at a level where it has enough food and clean water to survive. Our notion of sustainability and ecological footprint—indeed, our notion of world worth living in—presumes that humans will allow for, and themselves enjoy, enough room and resources for all species to live.

References Cited

1. Eldridge, N. 2005. The Sixth Extinction. ActionBioscience.org.
2. Crutzen, P. J. and E. F. Stoermer. 2000. The 'Anthropocene'. Global Change Newsletter 41:17–18, 2000; Zalasiewicz, J. et al. 2008. Are We Now Living in the Anthropocene?. GSA Today (Geological Society of America) 18 (2): 4–8.
3. Vitousek, P. M., H. A. Mooney, J. Lubchenco, and J. M. Melillo. 1997. Human Domination of Earth's Ecosystems. Science 277 (5325): 494–499; Pimm, S. L. 2001. The World According to Pimm: a Scientist Audits the Earth. McGraw-Hill, NY; The Guardian. 2005. Earth is All Out of New Farmland. December 7, 2005.
4. McKee, J. K., P. W. Sciulli, C. D. Fooce, and T. A. Waite. 2004. Forecasting Biodiversity Threats Due to Human Population Growth. Biological Conservation 115(1): 161–164.
5. Ohio State University. 2003. Anthropologist Predicts Major Threat To Species Within 50 Years. ScienceDaily, June 10, 2003.
6. International Union for the Conservation of Nature. 2009. Red List.

In Australia Wildlife Is Suffering Like It Is in the Rest of the World

Kelvin Thompson

In the following viewpoint Kelvin Thompson argues that Australia, much like the rest of the world, is suffering from overpopulation. Thompson cites specific examples of animal populations in Australia that have declined precipitously as a result of overdevelopment of lands and are now about to become extinct. Thompson asks readers to investigate his plan for decreasing population growth in Australia. He believes stabilizing the human population would stem the destruction of the country's natural habitats and wildlife. Kelvin Thompson was formerly a member of the Australian Parliament.

As you read, consider the following questions:

1. As stated in the viewpoint, how many Australian species are threatened by extinction?
2. How many bird species are at risk in Australia because of climate change according to Thompson?
3. What broad solution is Thompson proposing according to the viewpoint?

"The Impact of Population Growth on Wildlife," by Kelvin Thompson, July 15, 2011. Reprinted by permission.

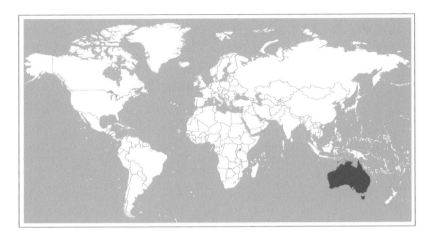

Some years ago there was a bumper sticker that said "At least the war on the environment is going well". It was a biting satire on the quagmire that had developed in Iraq. But the suggestion that we have declared war on the environment, that we have declared war on thousands of other species, is alarmingly close to the truth. While the human race grows exponentially, spreading into every corner of the globe, pretty much everything else is in retreat and decline.

Here are some examples of just how successful the war on everything else has been.

- Ten thousand years ago, the mass, the weight, all of the humans on the earth, plus all our pets, plus all the livestock we keep to feed ourselves, was 0.1% of 1%—one tenth of one percent—of the mass, the weight, of all the mammals on the earth. The rest of the mammals—elephants and tigers and rhinos and whales and kangaroos etc—made up 99.9% of the mass of all the mammals on the earth.

  By 200 years ago, humans, our pets and our livestock had increased from 0.1% to 10-12% of the mass of the mammals of the earth.

  Now, we, our pets and our livestock make up 96%—98% of the mass of the mammals of the earth. The poor old elephants and tigers and rhinos and whales and kangaroos and all the rest of the mammals have gone from 99.9% to just 2—4%.

- Since the Year 1500, around the world, more than 150 species of bird have become extinct. One in 8 species is now at risk of worldwide extinction, and 190 bird species are critically endangered. Of the common European birds, 45% are in decline, and 20 common North American species have halved in number in the past 40 years.

- One in two mammals are shrinking in number, and nearly one in four species is at risk of extinction. More than 3000 species are critically endangered, including land icons such as the African mountain gorilla and the Sumatran orangutan, and sea icons such as whales, dolphins and seals. Australia has 59 species—more than in one in five—threatened ; the mountain pygmy possum is down to 2000 and the Tasmanian Devil has suffered a 60% drop in numbers in a decade.

- Australia's coastal shorebirds are in freefall. Between 1983 and 2006 the Sooty Oyster-catcher, a resident shorebird, declined by 81% and the Whimbrel, a migratory shorebird, declined by 73%.

  One third of Australia's bird species declined between 1980 and 2000—examples include: Emu (50% decline), Banded Lapwing (60% decline), Wedge-tailed Eagle (40% decline), Black-Shouldered Kite (40% decline), Diamond Firetail (40% decline), Gang Gang Cockatoo (37% decline), Superb Lyrebird (30% decline), Brolga (27% decline).

- 45 species of Australian bird are regarded as at risk from climate change. Examples include the Wedge-tailed Shearwater—waters of the Great Barrier Reef which are too warm for its preferred food; the Fairy Tern, whose nests are now destroyed by foxes due to falling water levels in the drought stricken Murray, and the Mallee Emu Wren has lost more than half its population in 10 years to bushfires and drought.

The more there are of us, the less there is of everything else. I consider it a grotesque piece of arrogance on our part as a species that we think that we have a right to destroy everything else on our way to affluence.

Some species have prospered as a result of human activity, but the vast majority have not, and many species are now threatened with extinction.

In December 2005 the USA based National Academy of Sciences reported that human activities are leading to a wave of extinctions over 100 times greater than natural rates. According to the World Conservation Union, almost 800 species have become extinct since 1500, when accurate records began. The Alliance for Zero Extinction has identified a further 794 species on the brink of oblivion. These species are confined to 595 sites around the world; only one third of them have legal protection, and most are surrounded by human population densities approximately three times the global average. The country which has the world's worst record for species extinction turns out to be Australia. 27 mammal species, 23 bird species, and 4 frog species have become extinct over the past 200 years.

And the prospects for many other Australian species are not good. The Humane Society International says that land clearing has killed 4 billion birds, reptiles and mammals since 1972.

In November 2003 the Swiss-based World Conservation Union listed 12,259 varieties of animal, plant and water life as critically endangered. It noted that famous islands such as the Galapagos, Hawaii and the Seychelles are becoming ecologically and aesthetically barren as a consequence of human activities. Indonesia, Brazil, China and Peru have the highest number of endangered birds and mammals, while plants are most under threat in Ecuador, Malaysia, Sri Lanka, Indonesia and Brazil. Industrialisation, forest clearance and tourism are key culprits. In Columbia and Venezuela the spider monkey has been driven into smaller and smaller areas by urban growth, agriculture and cattle ranching. The population of the Giant Catfish in Southeast

Humans Are Destroying the Natural World

The Living Planet Report 2018 shows that between 1970 and 2014, vertebrate—mammal, fish, bird, amphibian and reptile—population sizes have been reduced by 60 percent. South and Central America have been hit particularly hard, suffering population declines of 89 percent.

The report is one of the most comprehensive global analyses of biodiversity, yet it does have its limitations. It only tracks vertebrates, sampling is not standardised across different biomes, and it ignores genetic diversity.

It's also worth noting that other global studies have reported different figures for biomass decline. A study in *Nature* looking at plant and insect species, estimates declines in species abundance of around 11 percent, and a study from Germany found a 75 percent decline in flying insect biomass in the 27 years up to 2016.

There are two main strands of argument when it comes to the loss of wildlife. The first is that the loss of nature is a necessary and acceptable consequence of human progress. Historically, our wealth has increased through exploiting the natural environment, and it has allowed us to live richer lives with more freedom of opportunity.

Counter to this, the argument runs that we can only push biodiversity loss so far before we threaten the life support systems of our small planet—

Asia's Mekong River has dropped by 80% since 1990 from over-fishing and dams blocking its migratory routes.

Reg Morrison put it like this: "the 300 million tonnes of humanity that the Earth currently supports has an appetite so voracious that the planet and its biota can meet our demands only by divesting itself of vast numbers of other energy consumers".

The biologist Edward O. Wilson calculates that humans have presided over the extinction of between 10% and 20% of Earth's prehistoric inventory of species.

The normal "background" extinction rate is about one species per million species each year. Human activity has increased extinction between 100 and 1,000 times over this level in the rainforest by reduction in area alone.

the capacity of the biosphere to regulate our climate, pollinate our crops, purify our water and decompose our waste. The biologist Paul Ehrlich once made the analogy that losing species in an ecosystem is like progressively removing rivets from an aeroplane: the plane may fly on for a while, but eventually it will fall out of the sky.

Such concerns have led to attempts to quantify "safe limits" of biodiversity loss, or so-called planetary boundaries that we must not cross else we risk a catastrophic tipping point. Although a compelling concept, there remains serious issues in implementing it. One is the uncertainty in the extent of biodiversity loss, the other is in the impact these losses will have on human livelihoods.

To make a comparison with climate change, many governments only committed to action after the likely economic impacts were quantified through meticulous analysis combining climate science and economics. Therefore, new approaches to more precisely quantify risk are urgently needed in order to galvanise action.

But even if we can ascertain the risks, will we actually be able to stop biodiversity loss?

"Tipping Point: Huge Wildlife Loss Threatens the Life Support of Our Small Planet," by Tom Oliver, Phys.org, November 1, 2018.

According to the United Nations Food and Agriculture Organisation the earth is down to its last 5% of tropical forest cover, and is losing that at a rate of over 200,000 square kilometres a year, with the rate of loss increasing. The world has entered the twenty-first century with little more than 10% of its original forest cover intact. According to anthropologists Richard Leakey and Roger Lewis all the forest cover will be largely gone by 2050.

In Australia many things are threatening our birds, plants and animals, but none more so than the loss of habitat, the loss of vegetation cover. If we're to save our birds, plants and animals, we have to put an end to habitat loss. What is the driver of habitat loss? Well that would be us. Population growth is the key driver of habitat destruction. Now the truth is that environment groups have been very reluctant over the years to raise the issue of population. There is no doubt that the issue of population is fraught with religious and racial overtones.

It takes courage to confront it, and I understand why people are reluctant. But I've said to other environment groups, and I say to you, that if environment groups are not prepared to tackle the root cause—population growth—you will be condemned to forever be fighting local battles to save remnant habitat—time consuming, energy-sapping battles which you often lose or are forced to make inadequate compromises. And even the things we think are saved and protected forever may not be.

One Sydney property developer has suggested that Sydney's magnificent ring of National Parks may be a luxury we can no longer afford. Never mind the obvious response that if we can no longer afford something, it sounds like we are getting poorer rather than richer as a consequence of population growth. The fact that such statements can be made shows that the only way we can guarantee that the beautiful bird, animal and plant life we are blessed with in Australia will live on, for the enjoyment and enlightenment of our children and their children, is to move to stabilize our population.

I have produced a 14 Point Plan for Population Reform which proposes that we stabilize our population at 26 million by 2050, rather than the 36 million we are presently tracking for, by cutting our net overseas migration to 70,000 per annum. This is not anti migration, it's not no migration, or no net migration. It's a return to the kind of migration number we had in numerous years in the 1970s, 80s and even 1990s. I encourage you to look at the Plan, which is on my website, and contact my office if you want to be on my population supporters database, which I have built up and which is campaigning for population reform.

To Protect Biodiversity, the World Must Practice Ecological Farming

Kumi Naidoo

In the following viewpoint Kumi Naidoo examines current farming practices and how they impact biodiversity. Naidoo argues that most common farming practices and corporate farming are harming the environment, which is affecting biodiversity and humans. Naidoo maintains a logical argument for ecological and sustainable farming as well as other updated farming techniques that would not contribute to climate change and therefore would help the environment. Kumi Naidoo is the secretary general of Amnesty International and formerly an executive director of Greenpeace.

As you read, consider the following questions:

1. According to Naidoo, what is our modern food system causing to happen?
2. What has climate change done to the cost of food as stated in the viewpoint?
3. How can ecological farming positively impact society, according to the author?

"The Food System We Choose Affects Biodiversity: Do We Want Monocultures?" by Kumi Naidoo, Guardian News & Media Limited, May 22, 2014. Reprinted by permission.

On today's United Nations biodiversity day, we are being asked to focus on small islands and their unique ecology and fragility in times of globally pervasive threats such as climate change.

But, the whole planet is a small island in the vast sea of space, capable of producing food for all as a consequence of rich biodiversity. That diversity is under threat, our actions can strengthen it or weaken it. Our agriculture systems can help mitigate climate change and feed us, or they can accelerate the change and contribute to hunger.

The food system we choose has a direct impact on which type of world we will have. It's the difference between a field that hums and is robust with life, or one which is dusty, dry and dead. It's the difference between a place where ecological farming has been used or where a cocktail of industrial chemicals has soaked into the soil where the same crop is grown, decade after decade.

Our current food and farming system is creating more and more of these dry, dead ends. It is agriculture characterised by three things: the industrial-sized growing of a single plant, or "monoculture", genetically engineered crops, and repeated toxic chemical infusions of pesticides and the application of synthetic fertilisers. All of these harm people and the farming ecosystems they depend on.

Just one example of the consequences of the current flawed agricultural system is the current catastrophic bee decline. Bees are being decimated in Europe and North America by the intensive use of chemical pesticides. In recent winters bee mortality in Europe (pdf) has averaged at about 20%. A third of the food that we eat every day depends on bees and other insect pollinators.

This dead-end road sees large multinational corporations persuading farmers to buy genetically engineered (GE) seeds based on the premise that they will increase yields, despite studies suggesting otherwise. Instead, they only increase farmers' indebtedness by failing to deliver the promised return on investment—turning them into slaves to a pesticide treadmill as superweeds develop. This is the ugly story behind the majority of the food we consume.

This cycle increases our dependency on fossil fuels and contributes to climate change, as the Intergovernmental Panel on Climate Change (IPCC) study recently reported. In fact, climate change affects this broken food system. Among other impacts, climate shocks cause food prices to rise, with deadly consequences in developing countries.

Climate change is estimated to have increased the amount spent on food worldwide by $50bn a year (pdf). Climate change is also making food less nutritious according to a study published in Nature, with important staple crops such as wheat and maize containing fewer essential nutrients like zinc and iron. Projections show that up to 21% more children globally will be at risk of hunger by 2050.

Industrial agriculture does not rely on diversification but on the standardisation and homogenisation of biological processes, technologies and products. It promotes off-the-shelf, one-size-fits-all solutions to food and farming around the world and in so doing undermines local and natural diversity, which are essential for resilience to climate change.

Ecological farming increases resilience to climate shocks. It is based on the diversity of nature to produce healthy food for all: diversity of seeds and plants; diversity of many different crops grown in the same field; diversity of insects that pollinate (like bees) or eliminate pests; and diversity of farming systems that mix crops with livestock.

Scientists from Wageningen University in the Netherlands, for example, recently found that certain beans greatly improve poor soils, increase productivity of maize when grown together and respond well to drought. They can be used for food, animal feed, and soil fertility. Researchers found that growing maize and beans at the same time increased farmers' income by 67% without the use of any chemical fertilisers.

Ecological farming also relies on the innovations of farmers that enable adaptation to local conditions. It's the redeployment of traditional knowledge to counteract the impacts of climate change. In north-east Thailand, jasmine rice farmers have been adapting to increased drought by finding creative ways to use water resources— stock ponds for storage and simple wind-powered pumps made with locally available materials—which have been shown to increase yields and provide a safety net when drought strikes.

Ecological farming effectively contributes to climate change mitigation. Industrial farming is a massive greenhouse gas (GHG) emitter. Agriculture, in fact, accounts for between 17% and 32% of all the emissions caused by humans, according to research for Greenpeace. Stopping chemical nitrogen fertiliser overuse and shifting to organic fertilisers (to increase soil fertility), improving water management in paddy rice production, and increasing agro-biodiversity through agroforestry are just a few examples of how ecological farming practices and diversity could directly contribute to GHG reduction and help agriculture reduce the effects of climate change.

Agriculture is now at a crossroads: we can pursue the dystopian dead-end road of industrial chemical-intensive farming or choose diverse and resilient ecological farming.

Governments, donors, philanthropists and the private sector must start shifting funds towards research to generate new knowledge on biodiversity-rich ecological farming and services to disseminate diversified practices that are locally relevant. We must reject the dead-end trap of industrial agriculture and choose instead a food system that celebrates biodiversity and is healthy for people and the planet.

In the United States, Brazil, and Indonesia Agricultural Practices Aim at Improving Biodiversity on the Farm

modernag.org

In the following viewpoint authors from Modern Agriculture take a look at farming and how it impacts biodiversity. The authors argue that farmers have an intrinsic respect for their land, and many use methods proven from research to protect their acreage. Specific practices are outlined that show progress in the United States, Brazil, and Indonesia toward an increased biodiversity on farmed land. Modern Agriculture is supported by the Monsanto Company, an agricultural biotechnology corporation.

As you read, consider the following questions:

1. How long have biodiversity improving practices been around in farming as stated by the viewpoint?
2. According to the author, what farming practices prevent soil erosion?
3. What are Brazilian farmers doing for biodiversity according to the viewpoint?

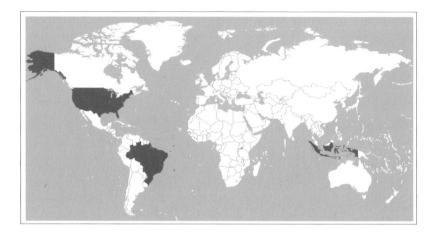

Farmers realize the importance of biodiversity, which refers to the variety of plants, animals and microorganisms above and below the soil within an ecosystem.

Farms are ecosystems in and of themselves. Each part, from the soil to the animals that live there to the crops themselves, has an important role to play. A change in this delicate system can have wide-reaching effects—so farmers understand that the decisions they make on their land must be considered carefully.

"Farmers are stewards of the land and the environment," said Dustin Spears, a farmer in northern Illinois. "We want to protect the land and the wildlife around us. We live out here, and we enjoy nature as much as the suburban and urban person looking for their weekend getaway."

There are many agricultural practices that farmers use to promote biodiversity. Many of the practices listed below have been around for at least 40 years, but they have seen an uptick in interest from farmers in recent years; those involved in agriculture have learned more about the importance of biodiversity on the farm. With more research under way into the benefits of the practices and technologies, we can expect to see more interest down the road. And that's good for biodiversity.

Farmers Are Practicing More Conservation Tillage

Tilling the soil is the practice of using a tool, like a plow, to turn up the soil. This practice helps to turn over the residue from the previous crop, provide loose soil to make it easier for seeds to take root, and disturb weed growth. However, this practice can increase the potential for soil erosion.

Conservation tillage minimizes the soil disturbance by using tools that turn over the soil lightly or hardly at all in some cases. The practice can leave some crop residue on the surface to lessen the opportunity for the soil to erode. Conservation tillage is increasing on farms: In 1983, only 17 percentof all U.S. farmland was in conservation tillage. In 2013, that rose to 63 percent. The main benefit of this method is that it aids in building organic matter for the soil, which helps to promote biodiversity.

Farmers Are Planting More Cover Crops

Cover crops are those planted by farmers in between the harvest of one cash crop and the planting of another. These crops, such as rye or radishes, can assist with soil conservation, keeping soil from eroding and returning nutrients and benefits to the soil for future crops. Cover crops also provide habitat for birds and insects, an important component of biodiversity. In a survey by the Sustainable Agriculture Research and Education Program (SARE) to more than 1,900 farmers, participants increased cover crops acreage on their farms by 30 percent each year because of the benefits they provide.

Farmers Are Conserving Land

In the United States, some farmers receive payments from the government to enroll a portion of their land in the Conservation Reserve Program, which encourages farmers to "remove environmentally sensitive land from agricultural production and plant species that will improve environmental health and quality." This land also serves as habitat for wildlife and can improve water quality.

Land conservation is truly a global effort. In Brazil, farmers are working with Conservation International and local stakeholders to implement better techniques to restore biodiversity in one of the most unique ecosystems in the world: the Cerrado. In Indonesia, another key biodiversity hotspot, farmers are participating in the Sustainable Agriculture Landscape project, which helps farmers meet the objectives of producing food and conserving habitat.

Farmers Are Planting Buffer Strips

Buffer strips are wide strips of land, usually grass, between fields of crops that help ease soil erosion and water runoff. These strips of land also play an important role in promoting biodiversity by providing a habitat for birds and animals. They are particularly beneficial in areas with hilly terrain.

Farmers Work with Conservation Districts and Environmental Groups

Many farmer and environmental groups connect to learn from each other on best practices to improve soil health, water quality, and air quality. For example, one such group is the Iowa Soybean Association, which works to "employ principles of cooperative conservation, planning, applied evaluation and adaptive implementation (to engage) partners in action-oriented, on-the-ground programs, projects and initiatives."

"We have improved how we farm over time, and while we have some work to do to continue to improve, I'm confident we will continue to balance the needs of producing food sustainably with the needs of the environment," said Spears. "For example, we want to use the least amount of inputs, such as pesticides, insecticides and herbicides as possible. We don't want to overuse inputs, as that may impact the environment, and it hurts our bottom line. We are much more precise with our applications. We'll continue to get better. It's as important to farmers as much as it is for consumers who eat the food we produce."

Habitat Destruction Affects Amphibians in Various Parts of the World

AmphibiaWeb

In the following viewpoint authors from AmphibiaWeb argue that amphibian populations are being lost because of habitat destruction and alteration. The authors note that amphibian populations are present in many different ecosystems, and that therefore their decline is caused by several different factors. These include global warming, drought, disease, invasive species, and habitat destruction. Scientists are working quickly on conservation efforts, but it may be too late. AmphibiaWeb is an online database created and maintained by The University of California, Berkeley, devoted to amphibian biology and conservation.

As you read, consider the following questions:

1. Amphibians are found in which two habitat types according to the viewpoint?
2. How is habitat destruction defined according to the authors?
3. What is the effect of habitat fragmentation on species as explained in the viewpoint?

H abitat destruction, alteration and fragmentation are probably the most serious causes of current and future amphibian population declines and species extinctions (Dodd and Smith 2003). Amphibians are found in a great variety of ecosystems from tropical rainforests to arid deserts (Stebbins and Cohen 1995). The general public often perceives amphibian habitat as being confined to wetlands and other aquatic environments, but surprisingly, a large number of species are entirely terrestrial (e.g., plethodontid salamanders and eleutherodactylid frogs; for a good overview of amphibian natural history, see Stebbins and Cohen 1995). This diversity in habitat requirements between species and even between life-stages of the same species emphasizes that we can not take a simplistic approach to amphibian conservation. In order to successfully conserve amphibians, we need a clear understanding of their varied life histories and habitat requirements. There are distinct differences between habitat destruction, alteration and fragmentation. Here we briefly discuss these differences and give examples as to how these factors adversely affect amphibians.

Habitat Destruction

Habitat destruction is defined as the complete elimination of a localized or regional ecosystem leading to the total loss of its former biological function (Dodd and Smith 2003). For example, habitat destruction is most obvious when amphibian habitat is drained, filled or cut and then converted into parking lots, housing developments or agricultural developments etc. A study by Davidson et al. (2002) found that habitat destruction due to urbanization has significantly contributed to the declines of the California red-legged frog (Rana draytonii). Although this species is usually found in or near aquatic habitats, adult frogs have been tracked moving up to 3 km over terrestrial habitat with little regard to topography. Encroaching urbanization into upland habitat, as illustrated in the picture below, may have devastating affects on adult movement and survival of this species.

Clearcutting alters habitats drastically and can have devastating affects on species richness and abundance. Petranka et al (1993) compared species richness and abundance of salamanders on six recent clearcuts with salamander densities in mature forest stands in the Appalachian Mountains. They found that salamander densities in the mature stands were five times higher than those in the recently cut plots. From these surveys, Petranka et al. (1993) estimated that timber harvesting in the Appalachian Mountains resulted in the loss of 14 million salamanders annually. The Food and Agricultural Organization's (FAO) (2007) biannual report gives global data on the state of the world's forest habitats(www.fao.org).

Habitat Alteration

Habitat alteration are changes made to the environment that adversely affect ecosystem function, although not perhaps completely or permanently (Dodd and Smith 2003). One example is livestock grazing, a serious problem for amphibians and other organisms that occur in aquatic environments. Livestock, such as cattle can effectively trample aquatic vegetation and cause accelerated bank erosion (especially in streams)and this can result in unsuitable habitat for amphibians. The picture below illustrates the effect of cattle on ponds. Notice that half of the pond is fenced off, keeping the cattle out. The vegetation is quickly reestablishing on the half of the pond that has been fenced off from grazing cattle, but the other side, which is still heavily used by cattle is barren. Fencing off portions of a pond to exclude cattle is one amphibian friendly management technique.

Habitat Fragmentation

Habitat fragmentation is a secondary affect of habitat destruction. The primary effect being the elimination of individuals or populations from the portion of the landscape that has been destroyed, and the secondary effect, habitat fragmentation, occurs when remaining populations are isolated because the links between habitat patches have been destroyed. Many amphibian populations exhibit a metapopulation structure, populations existing as an interconnected series of populations within a larger geographic area (Marsh and Trenham 2001). Metapopulation models predict that isolated populations are more likely to go extinct in the long run than populations that are slightly connected (Hanski 1999). Over time, habitat fragmentation can lead to the loss of genetic diversity which can affect a populationís ability to respond to environmental changes, confounding the effects of climate change, contaminants and introduced species.

Examples of habitat changes that may affect amphibian communities (modified from Dodd and Smitth 2003 and based on data from Hedges 1993, Beebee 1996, Mac et al. 1998 and Dahl 2000, reproduced with permission.)

Wetland Habitats

- 185,400ha of wetlands lost per year between mid-1950s and mid-1970s.

- 117,400 ha of wetlands lost per year between mid-1970s and mid 1980s.

- 155,200 ha of wetlands lost to urbanization and rural development between 1986 and 1997.

- 70-90% loss of wetlands in Connecticut, Maryland and Ohio between 1780 and 1980.

- 69% of pocosins of Atlantic Coastal Plain destroyed by 1980.

- 50% loss of everglades ecosystem by the early 1990s; the remainder greatly altered.

- 50 to 60% loss of wetlands in Alabama between 1780 and 1980.

- 54% loss of wetlands in Michigan, Minnesota and Wisconsin.

- 30 to 36% loss of wetlands in Arizona, New Mexico and Utah between 1780 and 1980.

- 91% loss of vernal pools and wetlands gone from California.

- 70% loss of ponds in Britain between 1880 and 1980s.

- 82% of marshlands destroyed in Essex County, England, between 1938 and 1981.

- Xenopus gilli has lost 60% of its wetland breeding sites in South Africa due to habitat loss.

Stream and River Habitats

- 98% of the original 5.2 million kilometers of streams in the continental United States have been seriously affected.

- 91% of river lengths in lower 48 US states developed by 1988.

- 33% of hydrological basins in northeastern United States affected by toxics: 63% by excess nutrients.

- 66% of the riparian forest in the United States has been destroyed.

- 85 to 98% of riparian forest in Arizona and New Mexico have been destroyed or severely degraded.

Terrestrial Habitats

- 0.01% of native grasslands remain in pre-European contact condition.

- 85 to 98% loss of oldgrowth forest in Blue Ridge and Cumberland Plateau provinces of Tennessee.

- 69% of Illinois forests present in 1820 are gone today.

- 60% of old-growth forest on Olympic Peninsula, Washington, is in patches of 40 h or less.

- 85% of coastal redwood forest reduced in California.

- 0.2% of original forest remains in Puerto Rico.

- Forest cover is only 13% of Cuba, 10% of the Dominican Republic, 5% of Jamaica and less than 1% of Haiti because of deforestation.

Literature Cited

Beebee, T. J. C. 1996. Ecology and conservation of amphibians. Chapman and Hall, London, UK.

Bickford, D. et al. (2008) Forgetting Habitat Loss in Amphibian Extinctions- Missing the Forest for the Disease. Accessed 4/11/2008.

Cooper N, Bielby J, Thomas GH, Purvis A (2008) Macroecology and extinction risk correlates of frogs. Global Ecology and Biogeography 17(2): 211-221.

Dahl, T. E. 2000. Status and trends of wetlands in the conterminous United States 1986 to 1997. U.S. Department of the Interior, Fish and Wildlife Service, Washington, D.C. 82 pp.

Dodd, C. K., and L. L. Smith. 2003. Habitat destruction and alteration: historical trends and future prospects for amphibians. Pages 94-112 in R. D. Semlitsch, editor. Amphibian Conservation. Smithsonian Institution, Washington.

FAO (2007). State of the World's Forests. Rome: Food and Agricultural Organization of the United Nations.

Hanski, I. 1999. Metapopulation ecology. Oxford University Press:i-ix, 1-313.

Hedges, S. B. 1993. Global amphibian declines: a perspective from the Caribbean. Biodiversity and Conservation 2:290-303.

Hijmans, R., et al. (2008). Worldclim. http://www.worldclim.org/ accessed 5/4/2008.

IUCN, Conservation International, and NatureServe. (2006) Global Amphibian Assessment. . Downloaded on 11 April 2008.

Mac, M. J., P. A. Opler, C. E. Puckett, and P. D. doran. 1998. Status and trends of the Nation's Biological Resources. Volumes 1 and 2. U.S. Geological Survey, Reston, VI.

Marsh, D. M., and P. C. Trenham. 2001. Metapopulation dynamics and amphibian conservation. Conservation Biology 15:40-49.

Petranka, J. W., M. E. Eldridge, and K. E. Haley. 1993. Effects of Timber Harvesting on Southern Appalachian Salamanders. Conserv Biol 7:363-370.

Stebbins, R. C., and N. W. Cohen. 1995. A natural history of amphibians. Princeton University Press:i-xvi, 1-316.

Sodhi NS, Bickford D, Diesmos AC, Lee TM, Koh LP et al. (2008) Measuring the meltdown: drivers of global amphibian extinction and decline. PLoS One 3(2): e1636. doi:10.1371/journal.pone.0001636

Stuart, S. Janice S. Chanson, Neil A. Cox, Bruce E. Young, Ana S. L. Rodrigues, Debra L. Fischman, and Robert W. Waller (2004). Status and Trends of Amphibian Declines and Extinctions Worldwide. Science 306 (5702), 1783. doi: 10.1126/science.1103538]

Overconsumption by the World's Wealthiest Will Lead to Ecological Destruction

Nate Bellinger

In the following viewpoint Nate Bellinger dissects an issue that is at the root of loss of natural ecosystems and therefore biodiversity. Overconsumption of goods by the world's wealthiest people is making it necessary to hunt down resources and thereby destroying ecosystems. People have and buy too much stuff that they don't need. At the time of this writing Nate Bellinger was a law student at the University of Oregon and on the executive committee of the Many Rivers Group of the Sierra Club.

As you read, consider the following questions:

1. According to Bellinger, what is a greater threat to the environment above overpopulation?
2. Which countries are most responsible for overconsumption as reported by the author?
3. As explained by the author how might sharing help decrease overconsumption?

When the population of the world reached seven billion people in October of 2011, many environmentalists used the occasion to renew their claims that overpopulation is the foremost environmental threat we are facing and will lead to ecological destruction and natural resource deficits. Overpopulation is definitely an important issue that we all should take seriously. However, in addition to overpopulation, an equal, if not greater, threat to the environment is overconsumption of finite natural resources. Here, I argue that overconsumption by the world's wealthiest people, and the negative externalities of this overconsumption, is one of the most pressing threats to our environment and something that we should all be paying more attention to and be thinking about ways to address.

Blaming overpopulation alone for the environmental problems that we are facing is a too simplistic approach; because the point at which the Earth is "overpopulated," or put differently, has reached its carrying capacity, necessarily depends on how many resources people are consuming. An overly simplistic example may help illustrate this point. Say there are 100 units of fresh water on Earth. If everyone consumed 20 units of freshwater, Earth's carrying capacity would be five people. If however, everyone consumed one unit of water, Earth's carrying capacity would be 100 people. Thus, population and consumption are inextricably linked—the more people consume, the fewer people Earth can support. If we did not consume so many resources, population would not necessarily be such a pressing environmental problem.

Overconsumption exists when resources are consumed at an unsustainable level as measured by the ecosystem's capacity. This is a problem because we live on a planet with finite natural resources. Some of the most critical natural resources that we rely on include freshwater, forests, topsoil, biodiversity, marine fish stocks, and clean air.

Today, we find ourselves facing a situation where overconsumption of natural resources is contributing significantly to deforestation, overdrawn rivers and aquifers, landscape degradation from mining, and other environmental problems. Furthermore, the negative externalities of this overconsumption are polluting rivers and oceans, contributing to climate change, and making people sick. It is time that we recognize overconsumption as one of the more serious threats facing our environment and begin thinking about ways to address the problem.

Overconsumption in Developed Countries

The world's wealthiest billion people, primarily living in developed countries like the United States, consume far more resources than is ecologically sustainable on average. We[2] buy cell phones (which we upgrade every two years); we have TVs, video game consoles, and cable boxes in multiple rooms in our house; we buy lots of cars[3] (which are much bigger than they need to be); our houses (which are also unnecessarily large) contain appliances such as air conditioners, dryers, dishwashers, and microwaves; and we are constantly buying new clothes, shoes, toys, and other household items. Consuming these products is not necessarily bad, but increasingly we are consuming these things excessively and are discarding and replacing things that are still perfectly functional. For example, two-thirds of appliances that are disposed of still work.[4]

In addition to all the "stuff " we consume, we also consume an inordinate amount of fossil fuels—coal, oil, and natural gas. These fuels power the cars and planes that enable us to travel around the world, heat and cool our homes, and provide us with electricity for our homes and for manufacturing. Again, this is not inherently bad, but we use far more fossil fuels than is necessary or sustainable, with perilous consequences for the climate.

We also consume many products that are used just once before ending up in a landfill. Every year, Americans use more than one billion plastic bags and throw away enough paper and plastic cups, spoons, and forks to circle to equator 300 times. In the United States, we consume 1,500 plastic water bottles every second.[5] We also consume tons (literally) of paper and cardboard, glass, aluminum, and other materials, which are used just once before being discarded (Recycling helps, but not consuming these products in the first place would be much better.) No matter what indicator is used, the fact is that the world's wealthiest are consuming a staggering amount of resources, far exceeding the sustainable level of consumption.

What is particularly troubling about overconsumption is the inequality in who is overconsuming. Unsustainable levels of consumption are generally found in affluent societies such as the United States, Canada, Europe, Japan, and Australia (countries where population growth is generally not perceived to be a problem). However, many of the externalities of this consumption are born by the poorest people. Carbon emissions, an indicator of fossil fuel consumption, provide a vivid example of this inequality—the world's richest half-billion people, 7% of the global population, are responsible for 50% of the world's CO_2 emissions, while the world's poorest 50% are responsible for just 7% of CO_2 emissions.[6] Americans have a particularly large carbon footprint—our per capita CO_2 emissions are second in the world among all major countries (Australia is number one).[7] The carbon emissions of one American today are equivalent to the emissions of 4 Chinese, 20 Indians, 30 Pakistanis, 40 Nigerians, or 250 Ethiopians.[8] These emissions are accelerating climate change, which affects us all but has particularly negative consequences on the world's poorest people.

In short, we are faced with an undeniable situation where a small number of people are consuming far more than their share of the planet's natural resources to the detriment of the planet and to the detriment of the poorest people.

It is worth noting briefly that overconsumption is not inevitable, and, in fact, has been increasing in recent decades. Although there are various factors contributing to this rise in consumption, the advertising industry is a major contributor. The average American is exposed to 3000 advertisements a day—and these ads tell us that we will be happier, sexier, and cooler with a new car, a bigger

TV, the latest clothing style, and the newest cell phone or iPod. In 2012, there were 36 companies that spent more than one billion dollars on advertising, primarily to convince people to consume more of their products.[9] The influence and success of advertising campaigns in encouraging people to consume more goods should not be underestimated.

What Can We Do About Overconsumption?

Admittedly, figuring out how to address the issue of overconsumption is challenging (though no more challenging than figuring out how to deal with the very sensitive and morally-charged issue of overpopulation). Here, I explore some preliminary thoughts on things that we as individuals and as the Sierra Club can do to address the issue of overconsumption; my hope is that this article will encourage others to think of their own ideas and ways to contribute, as well.

One of the most important things we need to do is to decouple the link between consumption and happiness. While advertisers spend billions convincing us that buying stuff will make us happy, there are numerous studies that support the notion that once people's basic necessities are met (mainly food and shelter), consuming additional products will not make you any happier.[10] The fact that you can't buy and consume your way to happiness is great news. It means that many people may not need to work so hard to make so much money in order to buy stuff that they don't need and won't make them any happier. Getting this message out is an important step that will hopefully encourage people to think more critically about why we unnecessarily consume so much stuff.

We also need to do more to educate ourselves and others about the true environmental impacts of our consumption. Sometimes this information can be hard to come by; at other times, it is out there, but we don't want to hear it. Before buying a new cell phone or flying on an airplane, we need to be aware of how that decision will affect the environment and think hard about whether the negative impacts are justified. If people had a better understanding of the true environmental impacts of their decisions, it might encourage them to consume less.

There are a number of lifestyle and cultural changes that we can promote to reduce consumption. One example is promoting a sharing economy, where people share various goods and services. For example, each household probably does not need its own lawnmower, vacuum cleaner, tool shed, or car. Instead, these products could be shared among households. This trend is catching on as more neighborhoods and communities are beginning to have tool- lending libraries and car sharing opportunities. Not only does sharing resources help reduce consumption, but it also tends to create a sense of community, which has many additional benefits.

Finally, we should be thinking about ways in which to incorporate the negative externalities of the goods and services we consume into their cost. One way to do this is through a carbon tax.[11] Such a tax would incorporate the negative externalities of carbon pollution into the cost of our decisions that result in fossil fuel consumption. If we were forced to pay for the true costs of all the fossil fuels we burn, we would very likely consume less. Whatever approach or combination of approaches is taken, it is extremely important for the sake of the environment and our overall well being to reduce the current levels of consumption in developed countries.

Conclusion

I believe that we, as Americans, the most proflagate consumers of natural resources in the world, have a responsibility and an opportunity to reduce our levels of consumption in order to minimize the negative impact we have upon the environment. Currently, we are consuming far more resources than is sustainable, with perilous consequences for the environment. Addressing the issue of overconsumption will not be easy, but it is critical if we want to leave a habitable planet for future generations.

Notes

2. I use the term "we" loosely because most Americans and readers of this publication will fall into the class of the world's wealthiest billion people.

3. The United States leads the world (excluding Monaco and San Marino, two small countries with a combined population of less than 70,000) in automobiles per capita.

4. Clean Air Council. (2013). Waste and Recycling Facts. Retrieved from http://www.cleanair.org/Waste/wasteFacts.html.

5. Scholtus, P. (2009). The US Consumes 1500 Plastic Water Bottles Every Second. Retrieved from http://www.treehugger.com/clean-water/the-us-consumes-1500-plastic-water- bottles-every-second-a-fact-by-watershed.html.

6. The Guardian. (2009). Consumption Dwarfs Population As Main Environmental Threat. Retrieved from http://www.theguardian.com/environment/2009/apr/15/consumption- versus-population-environmental-impact.

7. Pettinger, T. (2012). List of CO2 Emissions Per Capita. Retrieved from http://www.economicshelp.org/blog/6131/economics/list-of-co2-emissions-per-capita/.

8. The Guardian. (2009). Consumption Dwarfs Population As Main Environmental Threat. Retrieved from http://www.theguardian.com/environment/2009/apr/15/consumption- versus-population-environmental-impact.

9. Austin, C. (2012). The Billionaires' Club. Retrieved from http://www.businessinsider.com/ the-35-companies-that-spent-1-billion-on-ads-in-2011-2012-11?op=1.

10. For example, see Rosenbloom, S. (2010) But Will It Make You Happy? Retrieved from http://www.nytimes.com/2010/08/08/business/08consume.html?pagewanted=all&_r=0; Schwartz, B. (2012). Consumption Can Make Us Sad? Science Says We Can Be Happy With Less. Retrieved from http://www.thedailybeast.com/articles/2012/01/14/consumption- makes-us-sad-science-says-we-can-be-happy-with-less.html.

11. For more information about a carbon tax, see Parry, W. (2012). James Hansen, Climate Scientist, Suggests Price on Carbon. Retrieved from http://www.huffingtonpost.com /2012/10/11/james-hansen-climate-change-carbon_n_1959268.html; http://www.carbontax.org/.

Periodical and Internet Sources Bibliography

The following articles have been selected to supplement the diverse views presented in this chapter.

Nick M. Haddad, "Habitat Fragmentation and Its Lasting Impact on Earth's Ecosystems," *Science Advances*, March 20, 2015, https://advances.sciencemag.org/content/1/2/e1500052.full

Jeremy Hance, "Could Biodiversity Destruction Lead to a Global Tipping Point?" *The Guardian*, January 16, 2018, https://www.theguardian.com/environment/radical-conservation/2018/jan/16/biodiversity-extinction-tipping-point-planetary-boundary

IIkka Hanski, "Habitat Loss, the Dynamics of Biodiversity, and a Perspective on Conservation," NCBI, May 2011, https://www.ncbi.nlm.nih.gov/pmc/articles/PMC3357798/

Lida Ruishalme, "Monoculture: Do Intensive Farming and GMOs Really Threaten Biodiversity?" Genetic Literacy Project, July 14, 2017, https://geneticliteracyproject.org/2017/07/14/monoculture-intensive-farming-gmos-really-threaten-biodiversity/

Yasemin Saplakoglu, "Climate Change Could Drastically Change Ecosystems Around the World," LIVESCIENCE, August 30, 2018, https://www.livescience.com/63474-climate-change-vegetation.html

Paul Tolme, "The US Biodiversity Crisis," The National Wildlife Federation, January 30, 2017, https://www.nwf.org/Magazines/National-Wildlife/2017/Feb-March/Conservation/Biodiversity

University of Queensland, "Invasive Species and Habitat Loss Our Biggest Biodiversity Threats," Science News, December 10, 2018, https://www.sciencedaily.com/releases/2018/12/181210085919.htm

James Watson, "Half the World's Ecosystems at Risk from Habitat Loss, and Australia is One of the Worst," December 13, 2016, https://theconversation.com/half-the-worlds-ecosystems-at-risk-from-habitat-loss-and-australia-is-one-of-the-worst-64663

GLOBALVIEWPOINTS

CHAPTER 3

Why Is Biodiversity Important for Human Survival?

Loss of Biodiversity Directly Affects Human Health

Romulo RN Alves and Ierece ML Rosa

In the following excerpted viewpoint Romulo RN Alves and Ierece ML Rosa maintain that the health of humans depends directly on the vitality of biosystems and their biodiversity. Alves and Rosa examine how plants and animals are bioresources not only providing substances for traditional medicines, but also being effective ingredients for modern pharmaceuticals. The authors note that the effects of biodiversity on human well-being have gone largely unstudied. Further research will be important. Romulo Alves and Ierece Rosa are biology professors at Paraiba University in Brazil.

As you read, consider the following questions:

1. According to the viewpoint, what is one way human health is affected by biodiversity loss?
2. How does loss of biodiversity cause infectious disease as explained by the authors?
3. What is an example of a bioresource as reported in the viewpoint?

The interrelationships between society and nature, and the importance of environmental health to human health, have recently become widely acknowledged[4], and have drawn attention to the fact that biodiversity loss can have indirect effects on human well-being as well. By disrupting ecosystem function, biodiversity loss leads to ecosystems that are less resilient, more vulnerable to shocks and disturbances, and less able to supply humans with needed services. The damage to coastal communities from floods and storms, for example, increases dramatically following conversion of wetland habitats, as the natural protection offered by these ecosystems including regulation of water run-off is compromised. Recent natural disasters in Asia and North America serve to underline this reality[9].

Human health cannot be considered in isolation, for it depends highly on the quality of the environment in which people live: for people to be healthy, they need healthy environments. Agenda 21, which the governments of 185 countries adopted at this conference in Brazil, clearly spelled out the close link between human health and the environment; it also and highlighted the connection between poverty and underdevelopment on the one hand, and the connection between environmental protection and natural resource management on the other[8].

The implications of biodiversity loss for the global environment have been widely discussed, but only recently has attention been paid to its direct and serious effects on human health. Health risks are no longer merely a result of localized exposures to "traditional" forms of pollution—although these still certainly exist. They are also a result of broader pressures on ecosystems, from depletion and degradation of freshwater resources, to the impacts of global climate change on natural disasters and agricultural production. Like more traditional risks, the harmful effects of the degradation of ecosystem services are being borne disproportionately by the poor. However, unlike these more traditional hazards, the potential for unpleasant surprises, such as emergence and spread of new infectious diseases, is much greater[4].

Biodiversity loss diminishes the supplies of raw materials for drug discovery and biotechnology, causes a loss of medical models, affects the spread of human diseases, and threatens food production and water quality[10]. Its reduction has direct effects on the discovery of potential medicines.

[…]

In addition to the role biodiversity plays in helping people recover from illness, it also makes a significant contribution in preventing disease and illness, since well-functioning ecosystems can help protect human health. It is known that the poor suffer most from scarce or polluted water and air, and from diseases associated with disrupted ecosystems. One critically important service is the role ecosystems play in controlling the emergence and spread of infectious diseases by maintaining equilibria among predators and prey, and among hosts, vectors and parasites in plants, animals and humans. This protective function of biodiversity has only recently begun to be appreciated[20-23].

Examples of human infectious disease that can be affected by upsetting these equilibria include malaria and leishmaniasis through deforestation[24]; Lyme disease through changes in the number of acorns and in the populations of black-legged ticks, white-footed mice and white-tailed deer[25]; Argentine hemorrhagic fever through the replacement of natural grasslands with corn monoculture[26]; and cholera through increased algal blooms, secondary in part to warming seas and to fertilizer and sewage discharge[27].

[…]

Human activities are known to be crucial to transmission of some diseases. Forest clearance eliminates species that breed in water in tree holes (e.g., the forest Aedes species that transmit yellow fever) but provides favorable conditions for those that prefer temporary ground pools exposed to full sunlight (e.g., many of the Anopheles species that transmit malaria). Drainage of wetlands eliminates the marshy pools exploited by many species but can provide the open channels preferred by others (e.g., some important European vectors of malaria, and Culex tarsalis, a vector of St. Louis encephalitis)[29].

Bell et al.[30] remarked that one of the major lessons from SARS is that the underlying roots of newly emergent zoonotic diseases may lie in the parallel biodiversity crisis of massive species loss as a result of overexploitation of wild animal populations and the destruction of their natural habitats by increasing human populations. They also pointed out that to address these dual threats to the long-term future of biodiversity, including man, a less anthropocentric and more interdisciplinary approach to problems which require the combined research expertise of ecologists, conservation biologists, veterinarians, epidemiologists, virologists, as well as human health professionals is needed.

[…]

Plants and Animals as Bioresources

Plants and animals have been used as a source of medicines from ancient times[41-43], and even in modern times, animal and plant-based systems continue to play an essential role in health care[10]. Wild and domestic animals and their by-products (e.g., hooves, skins, bones, feathers, tusks) form important ingredients in the preparation of curative, protective and preventive medicine[44]. Additionally, a significant portion of the currently available non-synthetic and/or semi-synthetic pharmaceuticals in clinical use is comprised of drugs derived from higher plants[45, 46], followed by microbial, animal and mineral products, in that order[47].

The value of biodiversity to human health has been highlighted in literature[48], one of its most obvious benefit being the large proportion of the pharmaceutical armamentarium that is derived from the natural world. Over 50% of commercially available drugs are based on bioactive compounds extracted (or patterned) from non-human species[49], including some lifesaving medicines such as cytarabine, derived from a Caribbean sponge, which is reputed as the single most effective agent for inducing remission in acute myelocytic leukemia[50]. Other examples of drugs from biological sources include: quinidine to treat cardiac arrhythmias, D-tubocurarine to help induce deep muscle relaxation without general anesthetics, vinblastine to fight Hodgkin's disease, vincristine for acute childhood leukemias, combadigitalis to treat heart failure, ranitidine to fight ulcers, levothyroxine for thyroid hormone replacement therapy, digoxin to treat heart disease, enalapril maleate to reduce high blood pressure, and even aspirin [51,52].

A great number of these natural products have come to us from the scientific study of remedies traditionally employed by various cultures, most of them being plant-derived[53]. It is widely accepted that folk or traditional medicinal uses (ethnomedical information) of plants indicate the presence of a biologically active constituent(s) in a plant. In other words, folk or traditional medicinal uses represent "leads" that could shortcut the discovery of modern medicines. In fact, the results presented in an often cited work[54] revealed that from 119 known useful plant-derived drugs, 74% of the chemical compounds used as drugs have the same or related use as the plants from which they were derived. As pointed out by that same author, although the results do not mean that 74% of all medical claims for plants are valid, they surely point out that there is a significance to medicinal folklore that was not previously documented. Other papers on this subject [55-58] also attest to the important role of the traditional medicinal use of plants in modern drug discovery.

[...]

Ingredients sourced from wild plants and animals are not only widely used in traditional medicines, but are also increasingly valued as raw materials in the preparation of modern medicines and herbal preparations. Greater demand and increased human populations are leading to increased and often unsustainable rates of exploitation of wild sourced ingredients, with some wild species already threatened with extinction[65].

[...]

Conclusion

The interdependence between the sustainability of the environment and the sustainability of the human species needs full recognition and the development of new public health practices[91], which can increasingly translate into policies and actions the recognition that the sustainable use of finite natural resources is a major determinant of health.

[...]

The consequences for human well-being and health of disruptions to ecosystems are much more diverse and remain largely unstudied. It is therefore difficult to quantify current and future health effects of biodiversity losses and other changes to ecosystems. We are, however, acquiring new understanding of how the processes of forest clearance, agricultural practice, animal husbandry, river dams, and irrigation systems affect the emergence or the geographic and seasonal range of infectious diseases in humans[28].

The construction of a broad public health agenda is in order. Such agenda should evolve with an awareness of social, cultural, and political dimensions and should address values (equity, ethics), sustainability (regulation, financing, knowledge generation, knowledge management, capacity building), and the research environment[94].

The construction of regulatory measures will increasingly require the involvement of stakeholders, who must be made aware of the need for the conservation of the natural resource as a guarantee for its sustainable exploitation.

References

4. Millennium Ecosystem Assessment. Ecosystems and Human Well-being: Synthesis. Island Press, Washington, DC; 2005.

8. Lebel J. Health: an ecosystem approach. International Development Research Centre; 2003.

9. Pushpangadan P, Behl HM. Environment & Biodiversity: Agenda for future. ICPEP-3. 2005. http://www.geocities.com/isebindia/ICPEP-3/ICPEP3-S-2.html

10. Chivian E. Biodiversity: Its Importance to Human Health. Center for Health and the Global Environment. Harvard Medical School; 2002.

20. Anderson PK, Morales FJ. The emergence of new plant diseases: the case of insect-transmitted plant viruses. Ann N Y Acad Sci. 1994;740:181–94. doi: 10.1111/j.1749-6632.1994.tb19868.x.

21. Epstein PR. Climate, ecology, and human health. Consequences. 1997;3(2):2–19.

22. Daszak P, Cunningham AA, Hyatt AD. Emerging infectious diseases of wildlife: threats to biodiversity and human health. Science. 2000;287:443–9. doi: 10.1126/science.287.5452.443.

23. Ostfeld RS, Keesing F. Biodiversity and disease risk: the case of Lyme disease. Conserv Biology. 2000;14(3):722–8. doi: 10.1046/j.1523-1739.2000.99014.x.

24. Walsh JF, Molyneux DH, Birley MH. Deforestation: effects on vector-borne disease. Parasitology. 1993;106:S55–S75.

25. Ostfeld RS, Keesing F, Jones CG, Canham CD, Lovett GM. Integrative ecology and the dynamics of species in oak forests. Integr Biol. 1998;1:178–86. doi: 10.1002/(SICI)1520-6602(1998)1:5<178::AID-INBI3>3.0.CO;2-C.

26. Morse SS. Factors in the emergence of infectious diseases. Emerg Infect Dis. 1995;1(1):7–15.

27. Wenzel RP. A new hantavirus infection in North America. N Engl J Med. 1994;330(14):1004–5. doi: 10.1056/NEJM199404073301410.

28. McMichael AJ, Woodruff RE. Detecting the Health Effects of Environmental Change: Scientific and Political Challenge. EcoHealth. 2005;2:1–3. doi: 10.1007/s10393-004-0152-0.

29. Reiter P. Climate Change and Mosquito-Borne Disease. Environ Health Persp. 2001;1:141–161. doi: 10.2307/3434853.

30. Bell D, Robertson S, Hunter PR. Animal origins of SARS coronavirus: possible links with the international trade in small carnivores. Phil Trans R Soc Lond. 2004;359:1107–14. doi: 10.1098/rstb.2004.1492.

41. Lev E. Traditional healing with animals (zootherapy): medieval to present-day Levantine practice. J Ethnopharmacol. 2003;86:107–118. doi: 10.1016/S0378-8741(02)00377-X.

42. Yesilada E. Past and future contributions to traditional medicine in the health care system of the Middle-East. J Ethnopharmacol. 2005;100(1–2):135–137. doi: 10.1016/j.jep.2005.06.003.

43. Alves RRN, Rosa IL. From cnidarians to mammals: The use of animals as remedies in fishing communities in NE Brazil. Journal of Ethnopharmacology. 2006;107:259–276. doi: 10.1016/j.jep.2006.03.007.

44. Adeola MO. Importance of wild Animals and their parts in the culture, religious festivals, and traditional medicine, of Nigeria. Environ Conserv. 1992;19(2):125–134.

45. Farnsworth NR, Morris RW. Higher plants: the sleeping giant for drug development. Am J Pharm. 1976;148:46–52.

46. Farnsworth NR, Soejarto DD. Potential consequence of plant extinction in the United States on the current and future availability of prescription drugs. Econ Bot. 1985;39(3):231–40.

47. Soejarto DD. Biodiversity prospecting and benefit-sharing: perspectives from the field. J Ethnopharmacol. 1996;51:1–15. doi: 10.1016/0378-8741(95)01345-8.

48. Grifo F, Rosenthal J. Biodiversity and Human Health. Island Press, Washington, D.C.; 1997.

49. Grifo F, Newman D, Fairfield AS. In: Biodiversity and human health. Grifo F, Rosenthal J, editor. Washington, DC: Island Press; 1997. The origins of prescription drugs; pp. 131–163.

50. Chivian E. Environment and health: 7. Species loss and ecosystem disruption – the implications for human health. CMAJ. 2001;164(1):66–9.
51. Center for Biodiversity and Conservation (CBC) Biodiversity and Human Health: A Guide for Policymakers. New York, NY: American Museum of Natural History; 1997. http://research.amnh.org/biodiversity/acrobat/policy.pdf
52. Chivian E. In: Biodiversity and Human Health. Grifo F, Rosenthal J, editor. Washington: Island Press; 1997. Global environmental degradation and species loss: implications for human health; pp. 7–38.
53. Farnsworth NR, Bingel AS. In: New Natural Products and Plant Drugs with Pharmacological, Biological or Therapeutic Activity. Wagner H, Wolff P, editor. Berlin: Springer; 1997. Problems and prospects of discovering new drugs from higher plants by pharmacological screening; pp. 1–22.
54. Farnsworth NR. In: Biodiversity. Wilson EO, editor. Washington, D.C.: National Academy Press; 1988. Screening plants for new medicines; pp. 83–97.
55. Balick MJ. In: Bioactive Compounds from Plants. Anonymous, editor. Ciba Foundation Symposium 154. Wiley Interscience, New York; 1990. Ethnobotany and the identification of therapeutic agents from the rainforest; pp. 22–31.
56. Cox PA. In: Bioactive Compounds from Plants. Anonymous, editor. Ciba Foundation Symposium 154. Wiley Interscience, New York; 1990. Ethnopharmacology and the search for new drugs; pp. 40–47.
57. Farnsworth NR. In: Bioactive Compounds from Plants. Anonymous, editor. Ciba Foundation Symposium 154. Wiley Interscience, New York; 1990. The role of ethnopharmacology in drug development; pp. 2–11.
58. Cox PA, Balick MJ. The ethnobotanical approach to drug discovery. Scientific American. 1994;270(6):82–87.
65. Kang S, Phipps M. A question of attitude: South Korea's Traditional Medicine Practitioners and Wildlife Conservation. TRAFFIC East Asia, Hong Kong; 2003.
91. Brown V, Grootjans J, Ritchie J, Townsend M, Verinder G. Sustainability and health: supporting global ecological integrity in public health. Earthscan Publications; 2005.
94. Bodeker G, Kronenberg F. A Public Health Agenda for Complementary, Alternative and Traditional (indigenous) Medicine. American Journal of Public Health. 2002;92(10):1582–1591.

In the United States and Europe People Need to Spend More Time Alone in Natural Surroundings

Brad Daniel, Andrew Bobilya, and Ken Kalisch

In the following viewpoint Brad Daniel, Andrew Bobilya, and Ken Kalisch argue that modern-day schedules do not permit enough time for people to spend out in nature. As explained, and verified by research, the authors contend that people not only benefit from time in nature, but they realize that time alone is also necessary for optimal health. Brad Daniel is a professor of outdoor education at Montreat College. Ken Kalisch is an associate professor of outdoor education at Montreat College. Andrew Bobilya is an associate professor and program director at Western Carolina University.

As you read, consider the following questions:

1. According to the authors what is a problem with today's life for many people?
2. What do many people wish to have in their lives according to research by the authors?
3. What are two positive benefits of time spent in nature as explained by the viewpoint?

"Spending Time Alone in Nature Is Good for Your Mental and Emotional Health," by Brad Daniel, Andrew Bobilya and Ken Kalisch, The Ecologist, July 2, 2018. Reprinted by permission.

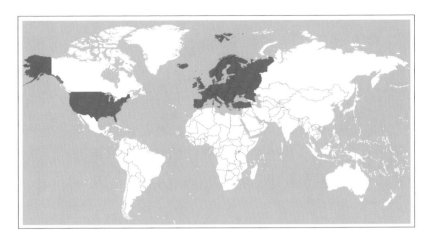

Today, Americans and Europeans live in a world that thrives on being busy, productive and overscheduled.

Further, they have developed the technological means to be constantly connected to others and to vast options for information and entertainment through social media. For many, smartphones demand their attention day and night with constant notifications.

As a result, naturally occurring periods of solitude and silence that were once commonplace have been squeezed out of their lives. Music, reality TV shows, YouTube, video games, tweeting and texting are displacing quiet and solitary spaces.

Alone, Not Lonely

Silence and solitude are increasingly viewed as 'dead' or 'unproductive' time, and being alone makes many people uncomfortable and anxious.

But while some equate solitude with loneliness, there is a big difference between being lonely and being alone. The latter is essential for mental health and effective leadership.

We study and teach outdoor education and related fields at several colleges and organisations in North Carolina, through and with other scholars at 2nd Nature TREC, LLC, a training, research, education and consulting firm.

Biodiversity

There is growing concern about the health consequences of biodiversity loss and change. Biodiversity changes affect ecosystem functioning and significant disruptions of ecosystems can result in life sustaining ecosystem goods and services. Biodiversity loss also means that we are losing, before discovery, many of nature's chemicals and genes, of the kind that have already provided humankind with enormous health benefits.

Biodiversity plays a crucial role in human nutrition through its influence on world food production, as it ensures the sustainable productivity of soils and provides the genetic resources for all crops, livestock, and marine species harvested for food. Access to a sufficiency of a nutritious variety of food is a fundamental determinant of health.

Nutrition and biodiversity are linked at many levels: the ecosystem, with food production as an ecosystem service; the species in the ecosystem and the genetic diversity within species. Nutritional composition between foods and among varieties/cultivars/breeds of the same food can differ dramatically, affecting micronutrient availability in the diet. Healthy local diets, with adequate average levels of nutrients intake, necessitates maintenance of high biodiversity levels.

We became interested in the broader implications of alone time after studying intentionally designed solitude experiences during wilderness programs, such as those run by Outward Bound.

Our findings reveal that time alone in nature is beneficial for many participants in a variety of ways, and is something they wish they had more of in their daily life.

We have conducted research for almost two decades on Outward Bound and undergraduate wilderness programs at Montreat College in North Carolina and Wheaton College in Illinois.

For each program, we studied participants' experiences using multiple methods, including written surveys, focus group interviews, one-on-one interviews and field notes.

Intensified and enhanced food production through irrigation, use of fertilizer, plant protection (pesticides) or the introduction of crop varieties and cropping patterns affect biodiversity, and thus impact global nutritional status and human health. Habitat simplification, species loss and species succession often enhance communities vulnerabilities as a function of environmental receptivity to ill health.

Traditional medicine continues to play an essential role in health care, especially in primary health care. Traditional medicines are estimated to be used by 60% of the world's population and in some countries are extensively incorporated into the public health system. Medicinal plant use is the most common medication tool in traditional medicine and complementary medicine worldwide. Medicinal plants are supplied through collection from wild populations and cultivation. Many communities rely on natural products collected from ecosystems for medicinal and cultural purposes, in addition to food.

Although synthetic medicines are available for many purposes, the global need and demand for natural products persists for use as medicinal products and biomedical research that relies on plants, animals and microbes to understand human physiology and to understand and treat human diseases.

"Biodiversity," WHO.

In some cases, we asked subjects years later to look back and reflect on how the programs had affected them. Among other questions, our research looked at participant perceptions of the value of solo time outdoors.

Our studies showed that people who took part in these programs benefited both from the outdoor settings and from the experience of being alone. These findings build on previous research that has clearly demonstrated the value of spending time in nature.

Intentional Solitude

Scholars in fields including wilderness therapy and environmental psychology have shown that time outdoors benefits our lives in many ways.

It has a therapeutic effect, relieves stress and restores attention. Alone time in nature can have a calming effect on the mind because it occurs in beautiful, natural and inspirational settings.

Nature also provides challenges that spur individuals to creative problem-solving and increased self-confidence. For example, some find that being alone in the outdoors, particularly at night, is a challenging situation.

Mental, physical and emotional challenges in moderation encourage personal growth that is manifested in an increased comfort with one's self in the absence of others.

Being alone can also have great value. It can allow issues to surface that people spend energy holding at bay, and offer an opportunity to clarify thoughts, hopes, dreams and desires.

It provides time and space for people to step back, evaluate their lives and learn from their experiences. Spending time this way prepares them to re-engage with their community relationships and full work schedules.

Participants in programmed wilderness expeditions often experience a component known as "Solo," a time of intentional solitude lasting approximately 24-72 hours. Extensive research has been conducted on solitude in the outdoors because many wilderness education programs have embraced the educational value of solitude and silence.

Time for Reflection

Solo often emerges as one of the most significant parts of wilderness programs, for a variety of reasons. Alone time creates a contrasting experience to normal living that enriches people mentally, physically and emotionally.

As they examine themselves in relation to nature, others, and in some cases, God, people become more attuned to the important matters in their lives and in the world of which they are part.

Solo, an integral part of Outward Bound wilderness trips, can last from a few hours to 72 hours. The experience is designed to give participants an opportunity to reflect on their own thoughts and critically analyze their actions and decisions.

Solitary reflection enhances recognition and appreciation of key personal relationships, encourages reorganization of life priorities, and increases appreciation for alone time, silence, and reflection.

People learn lessons they want to transfer to their daily living, because they have had the opportunity to clarify, evaluate and redirect themselves by setting goals for the future.

For some participants, time alone outdoors provides opportunity to consider the spiritual and/or religious dimension of life. Reflective time, especially in nature, often enhances spiritual awareness and makes people feel closer to God.

Further, it encourages their increased faith and trust in God. This often occurs through providing ample opportunities for prayer, meditation, fasting, scripture-reading, journaling and reflection time.

A Place Apart

As Thomas Carlyle has written, "In (solitary) silence, great things fashion themselves together."

Whether these escapes are called alone time, solitude or Solo, it seems clear that humans experience many benefits when they retreat from the "rat race" to a place apart and gather their thoughts in quietness.

In order to live and lead effectively, it is important to be intentional about taking the time for solitary reflection. Otherwise, gaps in schedules will always fill up, and even people with the best intentions may never fully realize the life-giving value of being alone.

Flora and Fauna Around the World Have Disappeared or Will Disappear in the Near Future

Earth Day Network

In the following viewpoint authors from the Earth Day Network paint a grim picture about the state of biodiversity around the globe. Using statistics collected from around the world the authors analyze the destruction done to the environment in the past and predict a troublesome future. Some of the loss is irreversible. Still, we can learn from our mistakes to prevent even more loss in the future. Earth Day Network is a nonprofit organization with a mission to educate people and activate a worldwide environmental movement.

As you read, consider the following questions:

1. What is significant about the figures 40 percent and 75 percent as reported in the viewpoint?
2. What poor excuse is used by some people speaking about this issue according to the authors?
3. How does fossil fuel use contribute to these problems as stated by the EDN?

There is no doubt that a vast number of animals and plants have gone extinct in recent centuries due to human activity, especially since the industrial revolution. The number of individuals across species of plants and animals has declined as well—in many cases severely—affecting genetic variation, biodiversity, among other issues.

All around the world, areas where humans exploit natural resources or undergo encroaching development all have the same outcome: a deteriorating natural environment. As a result of human action, ecosystems face threats such as unhealthy production and consumption; in today's interconnected world, it doesn't take much to see these unsustainable forces to take hold.

This is a trend that cannot continue. If ecosystems are too severely depleted, their ability to remain replenish, sustain our species, and meet human needs is drastically threatened.

Many of us have seen images depicting open prairies covered by massive herds of bison that no longer exist, enormous flocks of birds congregated in marshes and lagoons that have seen their numbers reduced dramatically, or beautiful and impressive animals such as elephants, giraffes, and whales, which—in many cases—are in danger of becoming extinct.

Other people have cherished memories of less imposing animals that nonetheless bring deeply felt emotions, such as the sound of thousands of frogs croaking in the middle of the night, birds visiting a backyard feeder year after year, or millions of bats flying to their resting place at dusk. Others might remember that when traveling by car through the countryside, their car's windshield ended up covered with hundreds of dead insects, which sadly was a signal of abundance that now hardly ever happens.

If you lived close to the ocean or spent much time there, you have probably heard that fish stocks have declined dramatically or read stories about whales, dolphins, and other marine mammals washing up dead on beaches, occasionally in large numbers.

In the last decades, we have learned countless stories of new species of plants or animals being discovered in tropical forests across the globe, giving us a sense of wonder and possibility. At the same time, millions of acres of natural forests are being destroyed every year.

Let's check some numbers:

- The number of animals living on the land has fallen by 40% since 1970.

- Marine animal populations have also fallen by 40% overall.

- Overall, 40 percent of the world's 11,000 bird species are in decline.

- Animal populations in freshwater ecosystems have plummeted by 75% since 1970.

- Insect populations have declined by 75% in some places of the world.

- About a quarter of the world's coral reefs have already been damaged beyond repair, and 75 percent of the world's coral reefs are at risk from local and global stresses.

- It is estimated that humans have impacted 83% of Earth's land surface, which has affected many ecosystems as well as the range in which specific species of wildlife used to exist.

Developed nations have seen benefits in economic growth not only from the exploitation of their ecosystems and species, but from the exploitation of the ecosystems and species of undeveloped nations as well. Currently, the biggest declines in animal numbers are happening in low-income, developing nations, mirroring declines in wildlife that occurred in wealthier nations long before. The last wolf in the UK was killed in 1680. For instance, between 1990 and 2008, around a third of products that cause deforestation—timber, beef, and soya—were imported to the EU.

Academics and others debate if we are already facing a new process of mass extinction, such as the ones the world has experienced over the millennia. But even if that is not the case, we know that thousands of species are endangered, and most land

and sea flora and fauna have seen their numbers severely reduced, with few exceptions.

Many species have disappeared already and many more are following the same path. As reported by The World Conservation Union (IUCN), there have been 849 species that have disappeared in the wild since 1500 A.D.; most strikingly, this number greatly underestimates the thousands of species that disappeared before scientists were able to identify them. Most troublingly, around 33% and 20% of amphibians and mammals are in danger of becoming extinct in the coming decades.

We also know that some people have argued that species have disappeared before and how the current decline is just part of a natural process. But this conclusion is way off base. All other processes of global mass extinction in the history of the planet happened because of a catastrophic natural event. They were not the result of human intervention, as is the case for the current mass extinction. According to Peter Ward from the University of Washington, what we are experiencing today is strikingly similar to the dinosaur-killing event of 60 million years ago, when a planet already stressed by sudden changes in its climate was knocked into mass extinction by the impact of asteroids. This mass extinction we are going through has been unfolding because of the intervention of a single species, us. Humans are having an outsized negative impact on all other species. Human activity has caused a dramatic reduction in the total number of species and the population sizes of specific species; thousand have already disappeared, and many more are threatened with extinction.

The marine extinction crisis is not as widely grasped as the crises in tropical forests and other terrestrial biomes. We do not know how many species are in the ocean as the bulk of marine species are undiscovered. Therefore, we do not know how many have disappeared or how many are in danger of disappearing. Furthermore, we are also losing species or unique types within a species (for example a type of salmon), before we even know of them.

We know that overfishing is a major global concern. Current assessments cover only 20% of the world's fish stocks, so the true state of most of the world's fish populations is not clear. Although, recent findings suggest that those unstudied stocks are declining, [20] and nearly three-quarters of the world's commercially fished stocks are overharvested and at risk.

Along with species extinction, the devastation of genetically unique populations and the loss of their genetic variation leads to an irreversible biodiversity loss. The evidence all points to the unfolding of a global tragedy with permeant consequences.

What Is Driving This Process of Extinction?

- Overexploitation of species either for human consumption, use, elaboration of byproducts, or for sport.

- Habitat Loss:
  - Habitat destruction: A bulldozer pushing down trees is the iconic image of habitat destruction. Other ways people directly destroy habitat include filling in wetlands, dredging rivers, mowing fields, and cutting down trees.

  - Habitat fragmentation: Much of the remaining terrestrial wildlife habitat has been cut up into fragments by roads and development. Aquatic species' habitats have been fragmented by dams and water diversions. These fragments of habitat may not be large or connected enough to support species that need a large territory where they can find mates and food. Also, the loss and fragmentation of habitats makes it difficult for migratory species to find places to rest and feed along their migration routes.

  - Habitat degradation: Pollution, invasive species, and disruption of ecosystem processes (such as changing the intensity of fires in an ecosystem) are some of the ways habitats can become so degraded they can no longer support native wildlife.

- Climate Change:
  - As climate change alters temperature and weather patterns, it also impacts plant and animal life. Scientists expect that the number and range of species, which define biodiversity, will decline greatly as temperatures continue to rise.
  - The burning of fossil fuels for energy and animal agriculture are two of the biggest contributors to global warming, along with deforestation. Livestock accounts for between 14.5 percent and 18 percent of human-induced greenhouse gas emissions. Those emissions come from cattle belches, intestinal gasses, and waste; the fertilizer production for feed crops; general farm associated emissions; and the process of growing feed crops. According to research conducted by the Worldwatch Institute's Nourishing the Planet project, animal waste releases methane and nitrous oxide, greenhouse gases that are much more potent than carbon dioxide. As people increase their level of income, they consume more meat and dairy products. The populations of industrial countries consume twice as much meat as those in developing countries. Worldwide meat production has tripled over the last four decades and increased 20 percent in just the last ten years. This information suggests that we should cut back on our consumption of meat and dairy. "The privilege we have over these animals, it would appear, now comes at a hefty price [to the planet]."

- The spread of non-native species around the world; a single species (us) taking over a significant percentage of the world's physical space and production; and, human actions increasingly directing evolution.

· The first factor is also known as the global homogenization of flora and fauna. Biotic homogenization is an emerging, yet pervasive, threat in the ongoing biodiversity crisis. Originally, ecologists defined biotic homogenization as the replacement of native species by exotics or introduced species, but this phenomenon is now more broadly recognized as the process by which ecosystems lose their biological uniqueness and uniformity grows. As global transportation becomes faster and more frequent, it is inevitable that species intermixing will increase. When unique local flora or fauna become extinct, they are often replaced by already widespread flora or fauna that is more adapted to tolerate human activities. This process is affecting all aspects of our natural world. For example, we grow the same crops anywhere in the world at the expense of the local varieties that in many cases disappear; introduce animals into places where they did not exist, and often do not have natural enemies, becoming a plague, such as rats introduced to the Galapagos Islands; or destroy other species that cannot defend themselves from the new predator, such as in Guam where over the years ten of Guam's twelve original forest bird species have been lost due to the introduction of the brown tree snake.Biological homogenization qualifies as a global environmental catastrophe. The Earth has never witnessed such a broad and complete reorganization of species distribution, in which animals and plants (and other organisms for that matter) have been translocated on a global scale around the planet.

· Over the last few centuries, humans have essentially become the top predator not only on land, but also across the sea. In doing so, humanity has begun using 25–40% of the planet's net primary production for its own. As we keep expanding our use of land and resources, the capacity of species to survive is constantly reduced.

· Humanity has become a massive force in directing evolution. This is most apparent, in the domestication of animals and the cultivation of crops over thousands of years. But humans are directing evolution in numerous other ways as well, manipulating genomes by artificial selection and molecular techniques, and indirectly by managing ecosystems and populations to conserve them, said co-author Erle Ellis, an expert on the Anthropocene with the University of Maryland. He added that even conservation is impacting evolution.

• Other: In countries around the world, policies have been enacted that have led to extinction or near extinction of specific species, such large predators in the US and Europe. Also, chemical products associated with agriculture or other productive processes have affected many species such as honeybees and other pollinators.

Worldwide Climate Change, Biodiversity Loss, and Nuclear Weapons All Threaten Human Society

Phil Torres

In the following viewpoint Phil Torres reports that according to the Bulletin of Atomic Scientists nuclear weapons are not the only major threat against human civilization. Torres maintains that biodiversity loss should be considered as a separate causal threat instead of being seen as a consequence of climate change. The author's compiled statistics do not paint an optimistic projection of what might be in store for humanity. Phil Torres is an affiliate scholar at the Institute for Ethics and Emerging Technologies.

As you read, consider the following questions:

1. According to the viewpoint, what are the three threats to human civilization?
2. What does the term "Big Six" refer to as reported by the author?
3. Which extinction event wiped out dinosaurs according to Torres?

"Biodiversity Loss: An Existential Risk Comparable to Climate Change," by Phil Torres, Bulletin of the Atomic Scientists, April 11, 2016. Reprinted by permission.

According to the Bulletin of Atomic Scientists, the two greatest existential threats to human civilization stem from climate change and nuclear weapons. Both pose clear and present dangers to the perpetuation of our species, and the increasingly dire climate situation and nuclear arsenal modernizations in the United States and Russia were the most significant reasons why the Bulletin decided to keep the Doomsday Clock set at three minutes before midnight earlier this year.

But there is another existential threat that the Bulletin overlooked in its Doomsday Clock announcement: biodiversity loss. This phenomenon is often identified as one of the many consequences of climate change, and this is of course correct. But biodiversity loss is also a contributing factor behind climate change. For example, deforestation in the Amazon rainforest and elsewhere reduces the amount of carbon dioxide removed from the atmosphere by plants, a natural process that mitigates the effects of climate change. So the causal relation between climate change and biodiversity loss is bidirectional.

Furthermore, there are myriad phenomena that are driving biodiversity loss in addition to climate change. Other causes include ecosystem fragmentation, invasive species, pollution, oxygen depletion caused by fertilizers running off into ponds and streams, overfishing, human overpopulation, and overconsumption. All of these phenomena have a direct impact on the health of the biosphere, and all would conceivably persist even if the problem of climate change were somehow immediately solved.

Such considerations warrant decoupling biodiversity loss from climate change, because the former has been consistently subsumed by the latter as a mere effect. Biodiversity loss is a distinct environmental crisis with its own unique syndrome of causes, consequences, and solutions—such as restoring habitats, creating protected areas ("biodiversity parks"), and practicing sustainable agriculture.

The sixth extinction. The repercussions of biodiversity loss are potentially as severe as those anticipated from climate change, or even a nuclear conflict. For example, according to a 2015 study published in Science Advances, the best available evidence reveals "an exceptionally rapid loss of biodiversity over the last few centuries, indicating that a sixth mass extinction is already under way." This conclusion holds, even on the most optimistic assumptions about the background rate of species losses and the current rate of vertebrate extinctions. The group classified as "vertebrates" includes mammals, birds, reptiles, fish, and all other creatures with a backbone.

The article argues that, using its conservative figures, the average loss of vertebrate species was 100 times higher in the past century relative to the background rate of extinction. (Other scientists have suggested that the current extinction rate could be as much as 10,000 times higher than normal.) As the authors write, "The evidence is incontrovertible that recent extinction rates are unprecedented in human history and highly unusual in Earth's history." Perhaps the term "Big Six" should enter the popular lexicon—to add the current extinction to the previous "Big Five," the last of which wiped out the dinosaurs 66 million years ago.

But the concept of biodiversity encompasses more than just the total number of species on the planet. It also refers to the size of different populations of species. With respect to this phenomenon, multiple studies have confirmed that wild populations around the world are dwindling and disappearing at an alarming rate. For example, the 2010 Global Biodiversity Outlook report found that the population of wild vertebrates living in the tropics dropped by 59 percent between 1970 and 2006.

The report also found that the population of farmland birds in Europe has dropped by 50 percent since 1980; bird populations in the grasslands of North America declined by almost 40 percent between 1968 and 2003; and the population of birds in North American arid lands has fallen by almost 30 percent since the 1960s. Similarly, 42 percent of all amphibian species (a type of vertebrate that is sometimes called an "ecological indicator") are undergoing population declines, and 23 percent of all plant species "are estimated to be threatened with extinction." Other studies have found that some 20 percent of all reptile species, 48 percent of the world's primates, and 50 percent of freshwater turtles are threatened. Underwater, about 10 percent of all coral reefs are now dead, and another 60 percent are in danger of dying.

Consistent with these data, the 2014 Living Planet Report shows that the global population of wild vertebrates dropped by 52 percent in only four decades—from 1970 to 2010. While biologists often avoid projecting historical trends into the future because of the complexity of ecological systems, it's tempting to extrapolate this figure to, say, the year 2050, which is four decades from 2010. As it happens, a 2006 study published in Science does precisely this: It projects past trends of marine biodiversity loss into the 21st century, concluding that, unless significant changes are made to patterns of human activity, there will be virtually no more wild-caught seafood by 2048.

Catastrophic consequences for civilization. The consequences of this rapid pruning of the evolutionary tree of life extend beyond the obvious. There could be surprising effects of biodiversity loss that scientists are unable to fully anticipate in advance. For example, prior research has shown that localized ecosystems can undergo abrupt and irreversible shifts when they reach a tipping point. According to a 2012 paper published in Nature, there are reasons for thinking that we may be approaching a tipping point of this sort in the global ecosystem, beyond which the consequences could be catastrophic for civilization.

As the authors write, a planetary-scale transition could precipitate "substantial losses of ecosystem services required to sustain the human population." An ecosystem service is any ecological process that benefits humanity, such as food production and crop pollination. If the global ecosystem were to cross a tipping point and substantial ecosystem services were lost, the results could be "widespread social unrest, economic instability, and loss of human life." According to Missouri Botanical Garden ecologist Adam Smith, one of the paper's co-authors, this could occur in a

---

Brazil's Overhaul of Protection Laws

Brazil's supreme court has upheld major changes to laws that protect the Amazon and other biomes, reducing penalties for past illegal deforestation in a blow to environmentalists trying to protect the world's largest rainforest.

Congress agreed to sweeping revisions in the law in 2012, including an amnesty programme for illegal deforestation on "small properties" that occurred before 2008 and reduced restoration requirements in others.

The changes effectively reduced deforested land that must be restored under previous rules by 112,000 square miles (290,000 sq km), an area nearly the size of Italy, according to a 2014 study published in the journal Science.

Environmentalists said the revised laws, known collectively as the forest code, would create a culture in which illegal deforestation is acceptable.

"This awards the guy who deforested, the guy who disobeyed the law," said Nurit Bensusan, policy coordinator at the Brazilian non-governmental organisation, Instituto Socioambiental.

"With this amnesty you create a climate that invites deforestation in the future. It creates the impression that if you deforest today, tomorrow you'll be handed amnesty."

Farmers and the powerful agriculture lobby argue that the new laws allowed for continued growth of the sector key to the Brazilian economy, without bogging it down in ajudicating crimes of the past.

---

matter of decades—far more quickly than most of the expected consequences of climate change, yet equally destructive.

Biodiversity loss is a "threat multiplier" that, by pushing societies to the brink of collapse, will exacerbate existing conflicts and introduce entirely new struggles between state and non-state actors. Indeed, it could even fuel the rise of terrorism. (After all, climate change has been linked to the emergence of ISIS in Syria, and multiple high-ranking US officials, such as former US Defense Secretary Chuck Hagel and CIA director John Brennan, have affirmed that climate change and terrorism are connected.)

The reality is that we are entering the sixth mass extinction in the 3.8-billion-year history of life on Earth, and the impact of this event could be felt by civilization "in as little as three human lifetimes," as the aforementioned 2012 Nature paper notes. Furthermore,

Rodrigo Lima, director of the agriculture consultancy Agroicone, said Wednesday's court decision brought legal certainty to rural producers by forgiving penalties for deforestation before 2008.

"If this apparatus had been struck down, for example ... everyone who submits information on the rural land registry could be fined at any moment even as they are complying with the [current] law."

The protections in question include those that apply to the Amazon rainforest, the majority of which lies in Brazil, which is vital to soaking up carbon emissions and countering climate change.

Deforestation in the Amazon fell in the August 2016-July 2017 monitoring period for the first time in three years, although the 6,624 sq km (2,557 square miles) cleared of forest remains well above the low recorded in 2012 and targets for slowing climate change.

Grace Mendonça, Brazil's attorney general, defended the 2012 revisions as constitutional saying they had been designed to strike a balance between environmental protection and economic development.

But many parts of the law designed to protect the environment have not been enforced, with measures such as a national registry of rural land still not fully implemented.

"Brazil 'Invites Deforestation' with Overhaul of Environmental Laws," Guardian News & Media Limitd, March 1, 2018.

the widespread decline of biological populations could plausibly initiate a dramatic transformation of the global ecosystem on an even faster timescale: perhaps a single human lifetime.

The unavoidable conclusion is that biodiversity loss constitutes an existential threat in its own right. As such, it ought to be considered alongside climate change and nuclear weapons as one of the most significant contemporary risks to human prosperity and survival.

Periodical and Internet Sources Bibliography

The following articles have been selected to supplement the diverse views presented in this chapter.

Doug Boucher, "How Brazil Has Dramatically Reduced Tropical Deforestation," *Solutions*, March 2014, https://www.thesolutionsjournal.com/article/how-brazil-has-dramatically-reduced-tropical-deforestation/

David Ferry, "It's Time to Let Certain Animals Go Extinct," *Outside,* April 25, 2017, https://www.outsideonline.com/2176276/its-time-choose-which-animals-we-let-go-extinct

Ary Hoffman, "Climate Change and Biodiversity," Australian Academy of Science, https://www.science.org.au/curious/earth-environment/climate-change-and-biodiversity

Nick Lavars, "How Biodiversity Loss Is Quietly Eroding the Potential for Life-Saving Drug Discovery," New Atlas, November 3, 2018, https://newatlas.com/biodiversity-loss-medical-possibilities/57057/

Megan Ray Nichols, "What Is Biodiversity Loss and Why Is It a Problem?" Interesting Engineering, June 4, 2018, https://interestingengineering.com/what-is-biodiversity-loss-and-why-is-it-a-problem

Matt Petronzio, "5 Major Threats to Biodiversity, and How We Can Help Curb Them," Mashable, May 23, 2015, https://mashable.com/2015/05/23/biodiversity-threats/

Julie Shaw, "Why Is Biodiversity Important?" Humanature, November 15, 2018, https://blog.conservation.org/2018/11/why-is-biodiversity-important/

University of California-Santa Cruz, "Variation Within Species Is Critical Aspect of Biodiversity," *Science News,* December 5, 2017, https://www.sciencedaily.com/releases/2017/12/171205120026.htm

Maryann Whitman, "Maintaining Biodiversity: Native Plants DO Provide Critical Ecosystem Services," *Wild Ones Journal*, Jan/Feb 2016.

GLOBALVIEWPOINTS

CHAPTER 4

How Can Biodiversity Be Preserved?

Are Zoos the Answer to Conservation Efforts?

Cristina Russo

In the following viewpoint Cristina Russo examines the issue of whether zoos are a valuable asset in the fight for conservation efforts of animals around the world. Russo argues that zoos have indeed changed since the days when they were pure entertainment and that they now function as sites for scientific research and education efforts. Specific examples demonstrate that education efforts in zoos might lead to interest in conservation. Christina Russo is a molecular biophysicist, science writer, and manager of a bioinformatics team.

As you read, consider the following questions:

1. What three functions do modern zoos carry out according to Russo?
2. How are animal demonstrations valuable in the zoo as explained by the author?
3. As reported by Russo, what do critics want to do with zoos?

"Can You Worry About an Animal You've Never Seen? The Role of The Zoo in Education and Conservation," by Cristina Russo, PLOS, March 11, 2013. https://blogs.plos.org/scied/2013/03/11/zooeducation/.

C an you worry about an animal you've never seen?

"He had black fur and a horn on his head," my sister said. She came to DC for a few weeks and spent many afternoons visiting our local zoo. After one of those visits, she hurried to Google Chat to report that a big tall bird was chasing her behind the fence of his enclosure. My sister described the bird as having long furlike feathers and a horn. She has never seen anything like that before and was genuinely curious. She was familiar with the belligerent bird's neighbours, the rheas (ratite birds like ostriches and extinct moas). Rheas are native to South America, as are we, and we've seen them before while growing up in south Brazil. "Mystery bird" was about to become a perfect example of zoo education.

What Justifies the Existence of Zoos?
Questioning the Goals Of Zoos

The role of the zoo has evolved to prioritise research, education, and conservation. Some people still condemn the existence of zoos based on zoo's past life of pure entertainment. It is true that zoos started as menageries and amusement parks, but they have come a long way since the late 1800s. Currently, laws protect wild animals and guarantee their welfare (e.g., Animal Welfare Act, Endangered Species Act, Marine Mammal Protection Act). Accreditation bodies make sure zoos and aquariums offer great care for their animals.

The field of animal research benefits from zoo experience. Zoo keepers, researchers, and vets have learned a lot about animal care as zoos evolved. Improvements in husbandry have led to increased longevity of animals in captivity. In his book At Home in the Zoo, published in 1960 and covering the previous thirty years on the Manchester Zoo, Gerald Iles mentions that "animals which were once either difficult or impossible to keep in captivity are not only thriving but breeding. Longevity records are constantly being broken."

Zoos have an essential role in conservation. Back in the 60's, Iles already said that "...the animals of Africa have been reduced by 80% within the last hundred years... and 600 species of animals are tottering on the brink of extinction." Currently, zoos have their own breeding programs to help in cases of dwindling populations. All efforts in captive breeding have led to increased research. Like author Jake Page put it, "many zoos have become places of rigorous scientific research… coupled with an active effort not just to preserve in captivity those creatures that are endangered in the wild, but… to understand, save, and replenish unique natural habitats." Besides breeding endangered animals (e.g. the successful golden lion tamarin breeding program, or the blackfooted ferret breeding program), zoos are also investing in displaying less popular animals.

Still, there are many people and organisations out there who dislike or choose not to believe in this new role of the zoo. People like Peter Batten, who in his book Living Trophies states that "primary reasons for zoo use are only remotely connected with learning."

Do Zoos Actually Educate?

A study at the Edinburgh Zoo tracks visitors who enter a primate exhibit "Living Links to Human Evolution Research Centre" in the Edinburgh Zoo. The exhibit is outfitted with a behavioural research centre, and on many occasions researchers are present and working with the primates. The study aimed to determine if watching the researchers had any impact on visitor experience.

The study followed visitors and measured their dwell time in the primate exhibit, in the presence and absence of primate researchers. They found that visitor dwell time increased in correlation to presence of researchers. Bowler and colleagues claim that "…parents were often seen explaining the research to their children … what was happening in the research room." But are visitors simply drawn by the "activity" (as opposed to passive viewing)? How do we know if the research observation is translated in education?

Another study aimed to identify the effect of animal demonstrations and of interpreters (the docent equivalent in zoos and aquariums). With a similar approach, Anderson et al. followed visitors and measured dwell time on Zoo Atlanta's Asian small clawed otter exhibit. In this study, researchers also surveyed visitors before and after they entered the exhibit. The survey attempted to find out if visitors' perceptions of otters changed after their visit. Did they actually learn?

Zookeepers and interpreters were present in the otter exhibit. They talked to the public about the otters, and showed their natural behaviours through demonstrations (see section about demonstrations below). Some visitors were offered a sea otter demonstration, a demonstration accompanied by interpretation (albeit read from a script), and some were not offered demonstration or interpretation (i.e. signs only). The study attempted to measure the effects of interpreters, animal demonstrations, and signs on visitor learning. They determined that the visitors spent an average of two minutes passively strolling the exhibit (i.e. with signs only and no human presence), compared with six minutes when animal demonstration was taking place, and eight minutes for animal demonstration plus interpreter. The survey results indicate that visitors preferred to watch the demonstrations. By comparing pre- and postvisit questionnaires, researchers believe that "visitors attending an animal demonstration retained large amounts of the content material weeks after having attended the animal demonstration."

Aren't Animal Demonstrations Just Entertainment in Disguise?

Most zoos offer animal demonstrations. I had a chance to watch sea lions on their training sessions. The zookeepers bring two of the animals out, while the public lines up to watch. The demonstration is in fact a training session for the sea lions: keepers reward the animals for certain behaviours, like rolling over, exposing their fins, allowing themselves to be petted. The sea lions receive rewards of fish and squid after they allow the keepers to treat them with eye drops, or rub their flippers. The goal of this training is not to amuse visitors, but to facilitate animal care. You can't force a 225 kg marine animal to roll over to ultrasound their abdomen. The training counts on voluntary animal participation and proves very effective for animal care and also for their mental stimulation.

Besides, it is a great opportunity for science education and for spreading a message of conservation. The keepers talk to the public about sea lions in their natural habitat, their anatomy, their innate differences from seals. They also mention that the two older sea lions at the zoo were rescued from the wild as pups when their mothers died as result of sea contaminants. The image of helpless orphaned sea lion pups in a polluted sea is a powerful one.

Educating By Creating Affective Connections

Jake Page mentioned that an affective connection with animals greatly helps conservation: "It is difficult to be concerned about the fate of an animal you have never seen. Even a twodimensional film representation of an animal does not have anywhere near the same effect as seeing one in the flesh, hearing it, smelling it. The usual response to such a reallife sight—whether in a zoo or in the wild—is emotional." Gerald Iles points to an extra benefit of zoo animals to education. According to Iles, animals are individuals with personalities, and allowing the public to see that will have an impact in their emotion: "the public, visiting a zoo, sees many kinds of animal. Each species conform to a set pattern, often based on facts gleaned at school. Elephants are just elephants; lions are just lions; bears are just bears. What the visitor often does not realise is that each animal is also an individual…all my zoo elephants were different from each other, and each one leaves me with a different memory." Another study reported on the "the positive effects of zoos on students cognitive and affective characteristics." As we've been saying here on SciEd, education can be maximised if there is an affective connection between learner and object: it's a moa at the mall, a marching penguin, and stumbling on learning opportunities.

Zoo critics will always exist. Many advocate for phasing out zoos, while offering no suggestion for what to do with the newly homeless animals. They even disapprove of the role of zoos in education. Peter Batten, the incredulous zoo critic, believes that "the zoo's contribution to education is minimal, ... and most people show no more than casual curiosity about its animals." As evidence for visitor's disregard for animals or for learning, he cites "years of hearing visitors call cassowaries 'peacocks', toucans 'fruitloops', tigers 'lions', and otters 'beavers.'"

At the zoo I've heard visitors call an ape "monkey," and a rhea "ostrich." It still does not change my belief that correct terminology is not necessarily an indicator of people's attachment to the animals. Visitors are not expected to arrive at the zoo knowing the names and species of all animals in its collection. And I'm sure they are leaving the zoo with more information than before they walked in. In fact, my sister saw the "black bird with a horn" (or what Batten's visitors called a "peacock") but left the zoo with the knowledge of a new animal. I'm sure she won't forget the rare sighting of the endangered cassowary,[which is considered vulnerable according the IUCN Red List of Threatened Species™, Moos]. That's an animal only found deep in New Guinea jungles, or in zoo conservation programs, where it helps researchers and visitors alike marvel at nature.

References

1. Anderson U, Kelling A, PressleyKeough R, Bloomsmith M, Mapple T (2003) Enhancing the zoo visitor's experience by public animal training and oral interpretation at an otter exhibit. Environment and behavior, Vol. 35 No. 6, 826—841

2. Bowler MT, BuchananSmith HM, Whiten A (2012) Assessing Public Engagement with Science in a University Primate Research Centre in a National Zoo. PLoS ONE 7(4): e34505.

3. Frynta D, Lis˘kova´ S, Bu¨ltmann S, Burda H (2010) Being Attractive Brings Advantages: The Case of Parrot Species in Captivity. PLoS ONE 5(9): e12568.

4. Kalof L, ZammitLucia J, Kelly J (2011) The Meaning of Animal Portraiture in a Museum Setting: Implications for Conservation. Organization Environment

5. Yavuz et al. Science and technology teachers' opinions regarding the usage of zoos in science teaching. The online journal of new horizons in education, volume 2, issue 4, 2011

6. Whitworth AW (2012) An Investigation into the Determining Factors of Zoo Visitor Attendances in UK Zoos. PLoS ONE 7(1): e29839.

Zoos Can Help Fight the Loss of Animals Around the World

Ben Minteer

In the following viewpoint Ben Minteer argues that zoos have a place as a force for preservation and conservation. Even though zoos have had success keeping some species from the brink of extinction, critics contend that it is cruel to keep wild animals contained for human amusement. Minteer argues that human behavior contributes so much toward loss of biodiversity that people need to fix this before asking zoos to do all the work for conservation. Ben Minteer is an associate professor of environmental ethics and conservation at Arizona State University.

As you read, consider the following questions:

1. What challenges face modern zoos according to the author?
2. Which species have been saved from extinction by zoos as stated by the viewpoint?
3. How does production of palm oil affect biodiversity as explained by the author?

"How Zoos Can Save Our Animals," by Ben Minteer, World Economic Forum, October 31, 2014. Reprinted by permission.

Today, many zoos promote the protection of biodiversity as a significant part of their mission. As conservation "arks" for endangered species and, increasingly, as leaders in field conservation projects such as the reintroduction of captive-born animals to the wild, they're preparing to play an even more significant role in the effort to save species in this century.

It's a task that's never been more urgent. The recent Living Planet Index report authored by the World Wildlife Fund and the London Zoological Society paints a disturbing picture: globally, on average, vertebrate species populations have declined 52% since 1970. Over-exploitation, habitat destruction and alteration, global climate change, and other pressures have created conditions that scientists now suggest signal a sixth mass extinction episode for our planet. It's an event rivaling the extinction of the dinosaurs.

The embrace of conservation by zoos, though, doesn't always sit well with their own history. The modern American zoo that emerged in the late 19th century fancied itself as a center of natural history, education, and conservation, but zoos have also always been in the entertainment business. This priority has led many skeptics to question the idea that zoos can play a helpful conservation role in the coming decades.

Zoos also face a formidable set of practical constraints—namely space, capacity, resources, and in some cases, expertise—that will continue to bedevil their ability to make a dent in the extinction crisis. It's also true that some of the most endangered animals are not the highly charismatic and exotic species that reliably attract zoo visitors. It's a challenge that might pit zoos' conservation priorities against their entertainment goals, and perhaps even their financial bottom line.

At the same time, wildlife protection does run deep in the history of zoos. The Bronx Zoo in New York, for example, led one of the earliest captive breeding and reintroduction efforts, helping to save the American bison from fading into oblivion more than a century ago. In the 1960s and 1970s, zoo conservation was energized by a burst of US federal policy-making focused

Elephants Under Threat in Tanzania

In Tanzania, the government, with support from WWF, has launched the country's largest ever elephant collaring effort to protect its dwindling elephant population. With almost 90 per cent of the elephants lost over the last 40 years in the Selous Game Reserve, a World Heritage site, enhancing rangers' ability to guard the remaining ones from poaching is essential to rebuilding the population.

In a project spanning 12 months, 60 elephants are expected to be collared in and surrounding the Selous. This will enable reserve management and government rangers to track elephant movements, identify and act against threats in real-time. The use of satellite collars is a proven effective measure to monitor wildlife movements and provide enhanced security.

The data collected through the collars will help teams predict where the elephants and their herds are moving to anticipate the dangers they may face, such as the risk of encountering poachers. It can also alert teams if the herd is heading toward community settlements to help move them away from farmlands and reduce the risk of human-elephant conflict.

In the past 40 years, rampant poaching of elephants for ivory has seen the population in Selous decimated, with numbers plunging to around 15,200 from 110,000. In 2014, UNESCO placed Selous on its List of World Heritage in Danger due to the severity of elephant poaching.

WWF is working with the government to adopt a zero poaching approach using a tool kit to protect the country's elephants and ecosystems in one of Africa's last wilderness areas. Zero poaching involves not just tackling poaching incidents but identifying the signs of poaching activities like snares and poachers' camps. On the ground, it involves action on several key areas; from ensuring there are enough properly equipped rangers to working closely with the local communities surrounding the protected area. It also includes working with prosecutors and judges to ensure that when poachers are brought to trial they face penalties that can act as a deterrent.

"Achieving a world free of poaching is an ambitious goal but just the kind of commitment we must deliver if we want to tackle the world's biodiversity crisis and ensure our future generations know and admire elephants and other species in the wild," said Margaret Kinnaird, WWF Wildlife Practice Leader. "Every year, on average, 20,000 elephants are killed for their tusks in Africa—this is unacceptable and must stop now."

"Unprecedented Collaring Effort Aims to Protect Tanzania's
Threatened Elephants," April 4, 2018.

on endangered species, especially the passage of the Endangered Species Act in 1973.

Many zoos went on to develop Species Survival Plans beginning in the 1980s, which coordinate breeding and population management programs for threatened and endangered animals among zoos worldwide. The goal is to create healthy and genetically diverse animal populations of these species across the zoo community, an effort that can ultimately aid the conservation of the species in the wild.

Reintroduction is a dicey business given the many biological and social factors that determine the viability of a population over time. Zoos' track records here are mixed—but the successes are real. In addition to the bison, the California condor, the Arabian oryx, and the black-footed ferret have been saved due in part to the efforts of zoos.

For animal rights critics, however, these outcomes don't offset what is seen as the basic injustice of keeping captive animals for human amusement. Earlier this year, the case of Marius the giraffe in the Copenhagen Zoo reignited the smoldering international debate over the ethics of zoos. A young and healthy giraffe considered a so-called surplus animal by the zoo managers, Marius was shot and his body was dissected before a public audience. The zoo argued that the decision was made on scientific grounds: Marius's genes were well-represented in the zoo system and so he was said to have no remaining conservation value. Animal advocates countered that zoos' noble conservation rhetoric masks a callousness toward the well-being of individual animals.

Whatever you think about the Copenhagen case—and it's worth noting that the American Association of Zoos & Aquariums disagreed with it—debates about the ethics of zoos shouldn't take place today without a serious discussion of our obligation to address global biodiversity decline. That includes thinking about how we influence the future of animals and ecosystems outside zoo walls with a thousand lifestyle decisions, from our consumer habits and energy consumption, to our transportation choices and what we put on our dinner plates. Take just one example, the mass production of palm oil. Widely used for cooking and commercial food production, its cultivation has resulted in severe habitat destruction and fragmentation in Indonesia. This in turn threatens the survival of orangutans in the wild.

There is a further challenge. As zoos become more engaged in conservation in the coming decades, the natural world will be further pressured and degraded by human activities. In many cases, nature preserves will likely require more human control than they have in the past in order to deliver the same conservation benefits. As a result, the boundary separating nature and zoo, the wild and the walled, will get even thinner. As it does, our understanding of what zoos are and what we want them to be—entertainment destinations, science centers, conservation arks, sustainability leaders—will also change. So will our idealized views of the wild as those places in nature that are independent of meaningful human influence and design.

Saying all this doesn't let zoos off the hook when it comes to caring properly for animals in their charge. We should also expect them to actually deliver on the swelling conservation rhetoric, especially when their entertainment and recreation interests run up against their expanding vision for biodiversity protection. But it reminds us of the scope of the challenge.

To paraphrase Dr Seuss, we all run the zoo.

To Protect Biodiversity Worldwide, Invasive Species Must Be Eradicated

Jacob Hill

In the following viewpoint Jacob Hill analyzes the worldwide problem surrounding invasive species. Hill provides surprising examples of just how destructive invasive species can be in different parts of the world. Hill explains how invasive species take hold, and why this is such a problem for biodiversity of native species of plants and animals. Jacob Hill is a field and conservation biologist with a special interest in threatened and endangered species and sea turtles.

As you read, consider the following questions:

1. What is a key factor is determining if a species will become invasive as explained by Hill?
2. What is ecological facilitation according to the author?
3. How are pythons threatening the biodiversity of the Everglades as stated by Hill?

One consequence of globalization is that in addition to people and products moving across the globe, wildlife has been transported as well. This practice of transporting animals from their native regions to new areas dates back thousands of years. The Roman Empire frequently brought back animals from foreign lands to use for entertainment in the Colosseum or used them for military purposes.[1] The practice was also a common part of European explorations of the New World, as explorers would bring back novel specimens to their home countries for zoological examinations or to arouse interest in future expeditions.

In many cases, the transplanted animal or plant does not thrive in its new environment. A lack of proper food sources combined with the wrong climate can make for a short lifespan for the animal in its new home. In other cases, however, the specimen thrives and is able to successfully reproduce and spread throughout its new habitat. When this happens, the plant or animal can wreak havoc on the new area and become an invasive species.

What Makes a Species Invasive?

Introducing a species into a new environment may have a variety of outcomes. An exotic or alien species is one that has been introduced to a new place, but does not necessarily have negative consequences. For example, many fish species have been introduced into the Great Lakes for sport fishing.[2] They have no documented negative impacts and provide recreational opportunities and a food source. However, when these alien species begin to have negative consequences in the new habitat, they are called invasive species. Invasive species may cause environmental harm, economic harm, or impact human health.

A key factor that makes many species invasive is a lack of predators in the new environment.[3] This is complex and results from thousands of years of evolution in a different place. Predators and prey often co-evolve in a phenomenon called the co-evolutionary arms race. What this means is that as prey evolve better defenses, predators in turn evolve better ways of exploiting prey. The classic example of this comes from the cheetah and antelope. Faster antelope survive better because they can better escape cheetahs. The fastest cheetahs then survive better because they can better catch the faster antelope. Neither species ultimately gains an advantage because they continually evolve in response to one another.

However, when a plant or animal enters a new environment, they will likely encounter predators who have not been evolving with them, which makes these predators unable to successfully exploit the prey. Defense mechanisms like venom, size or speed that have been matched by adaptation in predators are suddenly without match in the new environment. This can allow the species to proliferate rapidly as it no longer faces any predators.[2] Many insect or fungi that are invasive in the United States come from regions where native trees have evolved resistance to their effects. When these species enter the US, they find trees that have no resistance and they can decimate forests quickly.

Invasive species may also be able to exploit a resource that native species cannot use, which allows them to take hold in the new environment. Introduced into the Western United States, barbed goatgrass thrives in serpentine soils, whereas native plants do not normally grow in them.[4] This has given them a solid stronghold in the area. Combined with the fact that grazing animals do not like the taste of them, the grass has spread rapidly throughout California.

Some species also alter the environment in a manner that makes it more favorable for them, but less favorable for natives, which is called ecological facilitation. Yellow starthistle has also been introduced to the West Coast and secretes the chemical compound 8-hydroxyquinoline from the root.[5] This chemical harms native plants, which allows starthistle to increase its range as its chemicals wipe out native competitors.

Where Do Invasive Species Come From?

Invasive species may enter new environments through many routes. Some are transported to new places and established intentionally, but with unforeseen consequences. Beach vitex was planted in coastal North Carolina in the 1980's as an ornamental plant for coastal homes.[6] However, the plant began to overtake native species after it became established. The plant also does not have the extensive root system that holds sand in place as native plants do. As it spreads, the plants hasten dune erosion by removing plants that secure the sands of the dunes.

Some invasive species were actually brought in as unsuccessful attempts to control other invasive species. In the 1800's, rats that came to the Virgin Islands on ships infested the sugar cane fields on the islands, causing massive crop damage.[7] Farmers brought in mongoose as a predatory control for the rats. However, the rats are nocturnal and sleep in trees, whereas the mongoose are diurnal and cannot climb trees, so they were not successful at eradicating the rats. As a result, the islands now have two invasive species to contend with.

Other species are brought to different places intentionally but released accidentally, as happens sometimes with animals in zoos and aquariums. Lionfish are thought to have been introduced to the Caribbean when several of them escaped from a broken beachfront aquarium during Hurricane Andrew in 1992.[8] Sometimes people buy exotic pets and release them when they no longer want to care for them. This has been the case with Burmese pythons that are invasive in the Everglades.[9] These were once a popular pet because they are brightly colored and have an easy-going demeanor. However, they can grow up to 6 feet in the first year and live in excess of 20 years. A full-grown Burmese python can be up to 13 feet long and requires a specially-made enclosure and a large amount of food. This quickly becomes too burdensome for many owners, who then release them into the wild. As a result, a large population of these snakes now occupies South Florida.

A large number of invasive species have also been transported incidentally through shipping. The Great Lakes provide a good example of this. For millennia, the Great Lakes remained separated from other major bodies of water. When the St. Lawrence Seaway, a system of canals and dams, was built to connect the Great Lakes to the Atlantic Ocean, this waterway provided a conduit for invasive species to enter the area. This mainly happened through the discharge of ballast water.[10] Ballast water is used to weigh down empty ships and then discharged when ships enter a port in order to make weight available for cargo. The water is typically from the previous port where the ship was docked, and often contains living organisms from the area. By discharging ballast water into the Great Lakes when they arrive, ships have introduced more than 56 invasive species into the area.

In the 16th century, Spanish galleons also transported invasive species, but did so through ballast soil.[11] They would load the ship down with soil instead of water, but this soil also contained fire ants. As ships stopped at various ports along trade routes, dumping out the soil released fire ants into the areas, which were quickly able to colonize new places.

Many other examples exist of invasive species hitching rides on cargo to enter new habitats. For example, the fungus known as chestnut blight came from chestnut trees that were imported from Japan in the late 19th century.[12] The Asian tiger mosquito was introduced accidentally in tires shipped into the United States from Asia.[13] Naval shipworms entered the San Francisco Bay on cargo ships in the early 20th century and caused significant damage to piers and harbors.

Once they enter a new place, many different components of the habitat may facilitate their spread. Roads, for example, provide a pathway for invasives to move through new areas. The habitat alongside the road is clear of native vegetation, which makes it easy for fire ants to build mounds in this area.[14] When areas are cleared for grazing, the lack of native vegetation means less competition with existing species and can make it easier for invasives to establish themselves.

What Are the Consequences of Invasive Species?

Invasive species can have a number of negative impacts on the areas that they invade. Perhaps the most significant of these is the widespread loss of habitat. The hemlock woolly adelgid is an invasive insect from Asia that rapidly kills infested hemlock trees. In some parts of the Eastern United States, it is estimated that up to 80% of hemlock trees have been killed.[15] These forests represent important habitat for many animals and with crucial habitat gone, species that rely on them may face extinction. Similarly, the health of many forests is threatened by kudzu vines, introduced from Japan in the 19th century as an ornamental plant.[16] This plant was widely distributed across the Southeastern United States as a means of erosion control and as a food source for grazing animals. The vine soon became invasive, however, and can completely overgrow entire forests. In the process, it prevents sunlight from reaching the trees, effectively killing the forest. Additionally, the weight of the thick mats of vines on trees can cause trees to break and fall over. Its ability to quickly overgrow and destroy forests has earned it the nickname "the vine that ate the South."

Some invaders can physically alter the habitat in addition to destruction. 50 beavers from Canada were relocated to Tierra del Fuego, an archipelago at the southern tip of South America, in 1946 to be hunted for their pelts.[17] Since then, they have multiplied and now number in the hundreds of thousands. The trees in the region are not adapted to beaver activity as they are in North America, and most do not grow back after being gnawed by beavers. Portions of the formerly pristine forests now look like a bulldozer has plowed through them. Additionally, beaver activity creates ponds that flood portions of the forest. These bodies of stagnant water alter the nutrient cycle in forests and invasive plants thrive in them. Beavers also build dams in drainage ditches of grasslands and livestock commonly fall into them, where they become stuck and die.

Other invasive species may not destroy habitat but can have an impact by killing large numbers of endemic species. Burmese pythons, for example, are top predators in the Everglades. As such, they have decimated local mammal and bird populations.[18] Capable of consuming deer and even alligators, these creatures eat virtually any animal they encounter in the Everglades. A number of threatened and endangered bird species have also been found in the digestive tracts of pythons, prompting concern that they could drive some species toward extinction.[19] Lampreys in the Great Lake parasitize native fish. Because the native species have not evolved defenses to lampreys, they often die outright from wounds, or wounds become infected and eventually cause mortality.[20] Invasives can also threaten native species by outcompeting them for resources. Asian carp introduced into the United States outcompete native fish for both food and space, leading to large declines in native fish populations.[21] Invasive species are the second largest cause of species extinctions in the United States.[22]

Invasive species can also impact human health. Invasive zebra mussels accumulate toxins in their tissues like PCB's and PAH's. When other organisms prey on these mussels, the toxins are passed up the food chain and can also enter animals consumed by humans.[23] Ballast water from ships also sometimes contains harmful bacteria like cholera. Invasive animals can also be vectors for disease.

In addition to these impacts, invasive species can also have enormous economic costs. Zebra mussels in the Great Lakes can rapidly cover submerged surfaces, clogging up water intakes at water treatment facilities and power plants. Removing this invasive species costs an estimated $500 million annually in the Great Lakes alone.[24] Power companies spend an estimated $1.5 million each year to control kudzu vines growing on power lines.[16] Lampreys in the Great Lakes have decimated many fishery stocks to the point that they are no longer profitable.[20] In the United States, invasive species cost an estimated $120 billion annually in control methods and in loss of environmental resources.[22]

What Can Be Done to Deter Invasive Species for Specific Habitats?

Many strategies have been developed to stop the damage caused by invasive species and to prevention future invasions. An important component is educating people about the dangers of transporting wildlife to new areas. Many laws and regulations have also been passed to combat the future spread of invasives. Ballast water in tankers is required to be decontaminated before it can be released from the boat.[10] Laws have also been passed to restrict the exotic pet trade, such as banning the import of Burmese pythons in the United States.[25]

Promoting the harvest of invasive species is another widely used technique, although it has been employed with limited success. A python hunt in Florida in 2013 provided cash awards to people for killing pythons.[9] In Argentina, officials have tried to promote a market for beaver pelts and hunters were encouraged to hunt them.[17] People have also used the woody vines of kudzu to craft baskets and other items. A problem encountered with this strategy is that often the demand is not nearly high enough to make a discernible impact on invasive populations. In the case of pythons, they are extremely secretive and elusive, which makes them difficult to find them for eradication.

As with many environmental problems, continued research will yield insight into effective control measures. For example, research studies have been conducted to determine how effective traps are in catching pythons.[26] Genetic studies can also yield important information about how invasives have spread in an area and their potential to hybridize with native species.[27] Predicting how the geographic range of an invasive species will increase is important for preparing new areas that may be invaded. Much research has also been devoted to determining the most effective ways of removing invasive plants, whether through herbicides or through mechanical destruction of the plants. Using chemicals to kill sea lampreys in the Great Lakes during their vulnerable larval stages has been shown to effectively kill them without harming other wildlife.[20] While many invasive species may not ever by fully eradicated, increased awareness and research offer methods of preventing their spread and controlling the economic and environmental damage they can incur.

Sources

1. http://www.iridescent-publishing.com/rtm/ch1p1.htm
2. http://www.glerl.noaa.gov/pubs/brochures/invasive/ansprimer.pdf
3. http://evolution.berkeley.edu/evolibrary/news/141106_iceplant
4. http://anrcatalog.ucdavis.edu/pdf/8315.pdf
5. http://www.invasivespeciesinfo.gov/plants/yellowstar.shtml
6. http://www.invasivespeciesinfo.gov/plants/beachvitex.shtml
7. http://stthomassource.com/content/news/local-news/2006/03/05/mongoose-dem-trouble-territory
8. http://www.anstaskforce.gov/spoc/lionfish.php
9. http://www.washingtonpost.com/national/health-science/big-but-nearly-invisible-in-the-wild-officials-give-up-on-evicting-pythons-from-everglades/2014/03/16/58cab268-aa37-11e3-8599-ce7295b6851c_story.html
10. http://www.jsonline.com/news/wisconsin/how-invasive-species-changed-the-great-lakes-forever-b99297128z1-267010971.html
11. http://www.livescience.com/49866-how-fire-ants-spread-around-globe.html
12. http://www.ct.gov/caes/cwp/view.asp?a=2815&q=376754
13. http://www.invasivespeciesinfo.gov/animals/asiantigmos.shtml
14. Stiles, J.H. and R.H. Jones, Distribution of the red imported fire ant, shape Solenopsis invicta, in road and powerline habitats. Landscape Ecology, 1998. 13(6):335-346.
15. http://www2.ca.uky.edu/caps/hwa_hot_topic.asp
16. https://dnr.state.il.us/Stewardship/cd/biocontrol/25Kudzu.html
17. http://www.scientificamerican.com/article/argentina-and-chile-decide-not-to-leave-it-to-beavers/
18. Dorcas, M.E., et al., Severe mammal declines coincide with proliferation of invasive Burmese pythons in Everglades National Park. Proceedings of the National Academy of Sciences, 2012. 109(7):2418-2422.
19. Dove, C.J., et al., Birds consumed by the invasive Burmese python (Python molurus bivittatus) in Everglades National Park, Florida, USA. The Wilson Journal of Ornithology, 2011. 123(1):126-131.
20. http://www.glfc.org/sealamp/
21. http://www.nwf.org/wildlife/threats-to-wildlife/invasive-species/asian-carp.aspx
22. Crowl, T.A., et al., The spread of invasive species and infectious disease as drivers of ecosystem change. Frontiers in Ecology and the Environment, 2008. 6(5):238-246.
23. http://www.anstaskforce.gov/ans.php
24. http://www.copper.org/about/pressreleases/2009/pr2009_July_30.html
25. http://www.usnews.com/news/articles/2014/07/21/invasive-pythons-threaten-florida-everglades
26. Reed, R.N., et al., A field test of attractant traps for invasive Burmese pythons (Python molurus bivittatus) in southern Florida. Wildlife Research, 2011. 38(2):114-121.
27. Hunter, M.E. and K.M. Hart, Rapid microsatellite marker development using next generation pyrosequencing to inform invasive Burmese python-Python molurus bivittatus-management. International journal of molecular sciences, 2013. 14(3):4793-4804.

National and International Laws Aim to Protect Wildlife

National Anti-Vivisection Society

In the following viewpoint the National Anti-Vivisection Society analyzes the laws surrounding national and international animals and how these laws affect animal protection. The viewpoint lists and explains several acts of legislation and how these laws might spur conservation and improve biodiversity. The National Anti-Vivisection Society is an organization based in the United States that strongly disagrees with animal experimentation.

As you read, consider the following questions:

1. How does the ESA affect animal populations according to the viewpoint?
2. What is the Lacey Act and how does it protect animals as explained below?
3. Which countries have signed on to enforce the Migratory Bird Treaty Act?

There are many federal laws that protect wildlife, some with a very specific purpose, such as the Bald and Golden Eagle Protection Act, and others that cover a wide range of activities, such as the Lacey Act and the Marine Mammal Protection Act. One of the most important of these laws in preserving domestic wildlife is the U.S. Endangered Species Act.

The U.S. Endangered Species Act (ESA) embodies the desire of the federal government to conserve endangered and threatened species and to conserve their critical habitat. This law authorizes the U.S. Fish and Wildlife Service (FWS) to determine which species should be included on the lists of endangered and threatened species and when they should be removed. It requires the FWS to develop and implement recovery plans for each species on the list and to cooperate with the states to monitor how effective the plans have been.

A recent landmark decision by the FWS to include chimpanzees on the list of endangered species, marked the beginning of the end of invasive research on chimpanzees. The final rule, issued on June 12, 2015, now lists both wild and captive chimpanzees as endangered under the ESA. This ruling came as the result of a petition filed by a coalition of animal advocacy groups in 2011. At that time, chimpanzees had a unique position under the ESA as they were the only species with a split listing: chimpanzees in the wild were placed on the endangered list while captive chimpanzees were on the threatened list. Moreover, captive chimpanzees also had a special exception to their threatened species status that removed them from any protections under the ESA. In making its rule final, the FWS found that there is no legal justification for a separate classification for animals of the same species. Furthermore, the endangered species listing does not permit the special exception that was applied to the threatened species listing.

Another recent ruling of the ESA, on December 21, 2015, added lions to the list of endangered species. Lions were under consideration for this designation when Cecil was hunted and killed by a U.S. dentist after being lured from his preserve. As an endangered species, permits will now be needed to import any lion trophy, and the FWS has stated that it will exercise its full authority to deny future permit applications if an applicant has previously been convicted of or pled guilty to violations of wildlife laws.

There are additional federal laws and international treaties that impact wildlife, protect native populations and migrating birds passing through the country, and even committing the U.S. to help in the conservation of species in Africa and elsewhere.

- Airborne Hunting Act prohibits the harassment or taking of wildlife from any airborne craft (exceptions for federal and state officials and anyone granted a state permit).

- Antarctic Conservation Act conserves and protects the native mammals, birds, and plants of Antarctica and the ecosystems of which they are a part.

- Bald and Golden Eagle Protection Act prohibits the harassment of, trade in or taking of bald and golden eagles without a permit for scientific, exhibition or religious purposes. The regulations also provide for issuance of permits for the incidental taking of birds or their habitat for commercial purposes.

- Lacey Act enforces civil and criminal penalties for the illegal trade of animals and plants. It regulates the import of any species protected by international or domestic law and prevents the spread of invasive, or non-native, species. The law covers all fish and wildlife and their parts or products, plants protected by the Convention on International Trade in Endangered Species of Wild Fauna and Flora (CITES) and those protected by State law. It is unlawful to import, export, sell, acquire, or purchase fish, wildlife or plants that are taken, possessed, transported, or sold: 1) in violation of U.S. or Indian law, or 2) in interstate or foreign commerce involving any fish, wildlife, or plants taken possessed or sold in violation of State or foreign law.

- Marine Mammal Protection Act prohibits the taking and importing of marine mammals and marine mammal products.

- Multinational Species Conservation Acts serve to protect specific populations of animals through international treaties with other countries. These Acts include the African Elephant Conservation Act of 1988, the Rhinoceros and Tiger Conservation Act of 1998, the Asian Elephant Conservation Act of 1997, the Great Ape Conservation Act of 2000 and the Marine Turtle Conservation Act of 2004.

- National Wildlife Refuge System Administration Act requires that the Wildlife Refuge System management includes a strong and singular wildlife conservation mission, maintains the biological integrity, diversity and environmental health of the System, recognizes that wildlife-dependent recreational uses involving hunting, fishing, wildlife observation and photography, and environmental education and interpretation, when determined to be compatible, are legitimate and appropriate public uses of the Refuge System.

- Wild Bird Conservation Act limits imports of exotic bird species to ensure that their populations are not harmed by international trade.

- Wild Free-Roaming Horses and Burros Act aims to protect wild free-roaming horses and burros from capture, branding, harassment, or death.It gives the U.S. Bureau of Land Management and the Forest Service responsibility for protecting and managing wild free-roaming horses and burros as components of the public lands and maintain ecological balance on public lands, including the designation and maintenance of specific ranges on public lands as sanctuaries to protect wild horses and burros.

International Treaties

- Convention on International Trade in Endangered Species of Wild Fauna and Flora is the only treaty to ensure that international trade in plants and animals does not threaten their survival in the wild. A State or country that has agreed to implement the Convention is called a Party to CITES. Currently there are 181 Parties, including the United States. Each Party must regularly submit reports on how they are implementing the Convention, including information on any legislative and regulatory changes, as well as law enforcement, permitting, communications and administrative matters.

- Migratory Bird Treaty Act implements various treaties and conventions between the U.S. and Canada, Japan, Mexico and the former Soviet Union for the protection of migratory birds. Under the Act, taking, killing or possessing migratory birds is unlawful.

Biodiversity Offsets Are a Controversial Conservation Technique

Ariel Brunner

In the following viewpoint Ariel Brunner analyzes the topic of biodiversity offsets. These are attempts made by corporations and countries to repair the environmental damage they have caused by developing the land. Brunner presents the pros and cons of the use of biodiversity offsets. Brunner outlines the effects of biodiversity offsets from the point of view of BirdLife Europe, which is generally opposed to this way of conservation. Ariel Brunner is senior head of policy for BirdLife International.

As you read, consider the following questions:

1. According to Brunner, what is a biodiversity offset?
2. What is the mitigation hierarchy used for as explained by Brunner?
3. Do offsets always make sense according to the viewpoint?

Protecting forests and restoring wetlands are some of the actions companies and governments are taking to make up for biodiversity lost as a result of their development activities. These measurable conservation actions—designed to compensate for unavoidable impacts, on top of prevention and mitigation measures already implemented —are known as biodiversity offsets. The goal of offsets is to achieve no net loss and preferably a net gain of biodiversity on the ground in relation to species' numbers, habitat and ecosystem function.

Some of IUCN's member organisations have been involved in advising government and industry on offsets for several years. But with the rapid emergence of offsets, both voluntary and regulatory, there is lack of clarity on what they mean, how to design and implement them, and what mechanisms can be put in place to ensure they are used properly, and even more importantly, when offsets cannot or should not be used.

In response, IUCN has developed a draft policy on biodiversity offsets and is conducting a global consultation process seeking input. The deadline is 15 September.

Ariel Brunner, head of European Union Policy for BirdLife Europe, serves on the IUCN Biodiversity Offsets policy drafting committee. He shares his organisation's views on the issue.

Why does BirdLife care about biodiversity offsets?

BirdLife is dedicated to the conservation of biodiversity, and offsets have become a very contentious and popular aspect of biodiversity conservation in many parts of the world. If done right, offsets can play a useful role in conservation, but if done wrong, they can undermine conservation efforts.

Are BirdLife's programmes affected by biodiversity offsets in countries where it works?

Yes, of course. For example, in recent years, there has been a lively debate around the EU No Net Loss Initiative and offsets are part of that discussion. In the EU, legislation around the Natura 2000 sites—which are often important bird areas—includes offsets, or rather compensation of any damage remaining when development projects are authorised for reasons of overriding public interest. In other areas of the world, countries and companies are already implementing offsets, so this impacts a lot of places where we work.

What is the relationship between biodiversity offsets and the mitigation hierarchy in important bird areas?

It is really important to understand that a stand-alone discussion about biodiversity offsets does not make any sense. If you are trying to undertake a new development project, and there is strict legislation that says you cannot destroy certain habitats, you might be stopped right there. Or under certain circumstances and conditions, you might be allowed to compensate for any damage caused by using offsets, in other words, restoring and/or conserving biodiversity elsewhere.

But it makes no sense to approach biodiversity offsets from outside the mitigation hierarchy. The mitigation hierarchy is a sound framework to any form of planning that says, first of all, you should try to avoid any damage. Then, if you can't avoid, you should at least mitigate the damage and build the project in a way that creates the minimal amount of disruption.

For example, if you are trying to build a railway though a biologically important area that could prevent animals from migrating, then you might need to build an overpass so the animals can still use the land with minimal disruption.

After thoroughly applying all the steps of the mitigation hierarchy—which is an established tool used to help manage biodiversity risk—there may still be a decision to develop based on public interest or the needs of society. Then, even if the development is in the best place and built in the best way, but will still cause damage, you need to reduce the overall damage by taking conservation action and ensuring the development will improve similar habitats and species and maintain ecological functionality.

What is the general feeling across the BirdLife network about offsets?

BirdLife is quite wary of offsets in general. We recognise that offsets can play a role within the mitigation hierarchy, in some cases. But I think there is widespread worry in the biodiversity family about this current 'fashion' for offsets, which tries to present offsets as a stand-alone solution and this takes away the emphasis on avoidance. This is dangerous because it risks facilitating inappropriate development that should not happen in certain places. So, many BirdLife partners are engaging in offsets schemes, but only when they believe it can play a positive role and only when they are an integral part of a sound avoidance framework.

Given your experience working on policy issues across Europe, what are some of the current discussions on biodiversity offsets and a "no net loss" approach?

The biodiversity offsets discussion is controversial because some governments are pushing for offsets as a way to "speed up development", so basically as a way to undermine overall land planning and allow harmful development on protected land. This has generated a lot of opposition.

On the other hand, certain forms of offsets, such as compensation enshrined in the EU Habitats Directive, are clearly framed in a solid mitigation hierarchy process, which means certain species and sites of concern cannot be damaged. There are also very variable experiences with offsets as part of national legislation.

Some European countries have biodiversity offsets written into their legislation. One thing that is clearly important in the European context is the level of governance in a country or region. Where you have strong land planning and regional authorities, who can assess plans, monitor and refuse applications if necessary, offsets can play a positive role because this type of oversight can ensure residual damage is compensated.

Where governance is weak and dubious, and development projects get approved because of corruption or incompetence, offsets might be environmentally damaging.

What could IUCN learn from biodiversity offset experiences to date and what pitfalls should it try to avoid in regards to this policy?

The most important thing from my point of view is for IUCN to take away the specific focus on biodiversity offsets and put it on avoidance and mitigation. As long as we consider offsets as a stand-alone policy, we risk being misunderstood or even manipulated.

As a world authority on conservation, IUCN needs to promote sound land planning and licensing procedures that are based on the mitigation hierarchy. This would be a service to the conservation community. Then, all of the technical advice on how to handle offsets would be useful because it would sit within a sound framework.

One of the sensitivities around the offsets debate, which is less of an issue in Europe than in other parts of the world, concerns the potential social implications. One of the fears is that offsets could trample over the rights of local communities and be used to remove people from their land. The IUCN Biodiversity Offsets policy needs to recommend that offsets are developed following a Rights-based Approach.

If and when this policy is approved, what should IUCN do with it?

It will be important to share the new policy with both governments and investors, and ask them to bring their legislation, policies and codes of conduct into line with the policy. This means they should adhere to sound land planning and the mitigation hierarchy in the development and licensing of large-scale projects that are damaging to biodiversity. Decision makers will take notice of an IUCN global standard and this is why IUCN has a big responsibility.

In Borneo and Sumatra Orangutans Are Endangered

Orang Utan Republik Foundation

In the following excerpted viewpoint, authors from the Orang Utan Republik Foundation contend that orangutans, which once were numerous in their habitats, are now suffering as a species. The authors analyze the many reasons why the Bornean and Sumatran animals are losing ground and are endangered. The Orang Utan Republik Foundation is an organization which aims to save the wild orangutans of Indonesia.

As you read, consider the following questions:

1. According to this viewpoint article how many species of orangutan exist today?
2. What are two reasons why orangutan numbers are decreasing as explained by the author?
3. How do people pose a threat to orangutans as stated by the author?

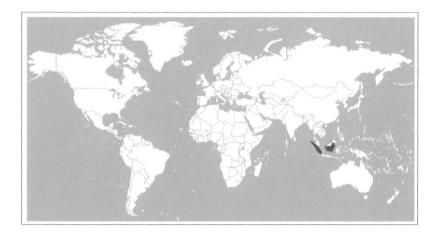

Orangutans are the only non-human great ape found in Asia, and were once widespread throughout most of the southeast of the continent, and even as far as southern China. Today, two species of orangutan exist, on the island of Borneo, which is shared between Indonesia, Malaysia and Brunei-Darussalam, and the wholly Indonesian island of Sumatra. Previously considered endangered in Borneo (now critically endangered as of 2016), where most recent estimates put the population at around 55,000, OURF has focused its efforts on the critically endangered population in Sumatra, which numbers around 14,500 (as of 2016).

Sumatra is an island in western Indonesia, and the sixth largest island in the world, with a population of around 45,000,000 people. Lying in the Pacific "Ring of Fire," Sumatra has been both blessed and cursed by extreme volcanic activity, which has endowed the island with fertile land and abundant tropical forests. Home to 580 bird species and 201 mammal species, 9 of them endemic to the island (WWF, 2008), Sumatra is made up of dozens of ethnic groups, who speak 52 different languages between them. Although strong local cultures and customs still exist, Islam is today the dominant religion.

Like most of Indonesia, Sumatra was once covered in tropical forests, and orangutans could be found throughout the island. Smaller, lighter colored and generally more social than the better known Bornean orangutan, today the Sumatran orangutan is found only in the island's northern parts. Legal and illegal logging, large-scale forest conversion, mining, and development brought about the extinction of southern populations and continue to fragment the remaining populations. Satellite imagery shows Sumatra has lost 48% of its natural forest cover since 1985 (WFF, 2008), and it is estimated that up to 800 orangutans are being lost every year as a result of habitat destruction and hunting. With a population of just a few thousand, if the current rate of decline continues, orangutans will be extinct as a genetically viable species in Sumatra within just 10 years.

A population of 14,500 can often sound large, particularly when compared to the 400 wild Sumatran tigers still surviving, or the 700 or so mountain gorillas of central Africa. However, in context, the figure is frighteningly low. Orangutans have the longest birth interval of any land mammal, females giving birth to one young every 6-8 years, from the age of 15, and usually producing no more than 3-4 offspring in their lifetime. With such a low birth rate, they are particularly vulnerable to hunting pressure or any kind of habitat destruction. Making the Sumatran orangutan crisis even more urgent is the fact that all of the orangutans in Sumatra are scattered throughout small patches of forest, all in the north of the island, all surrounded by human settlements and plantations, all isolated from neighboring populations, and all currently under serious threat of habitat conversion.

[...]

Threats to Orangutans

At the turn of the century, orangutan populations in Borneo and Sumatra numbered in the hundreds of thousands, inhabiting endless expanses of untouched tropical rainforest. Today, the situation couldn't be more different. Large scale logging and rampant plantation expansion has seen both forest habitat and orangutan numbers plummet drastically.

[...]

Bornean Orangutan Crisis

Surrounded by the South China Sea to the north and northwest, the Sulu Sea to the northeast, the Celebes Sea and the Makassar Strait to the east, and the Java Sea and Karimata Strait to the south, Borneo is, at 743,330 Km^2, the world's third largest island, and lies to the east of Sumatra. Borneo is divided between three countries; the state of Brunei-Darussalam, the Malaysian states of Sarawak and Sabah, and the Indonesian territory of Kalimantan, and has a human population of around 16,000,000, with the majority of settlements and cities lying near to, or along, the coastline or Borneo's extensive river system (Smith, 2007).

Like Sumatra, Borneo is extraordinarily rich in biodiversity. The major forest type throughout the island is evergreen lowland diptercarp rainforest, with hill diptercarp, mangrove, freshwater, peat swamp, ironwood, heathland and montane forests all also found (Rautner at al, 2005), and harbouring 3,000 species of trees, 15,000 species of flowering plants, 221 species of terrestrial mammals, including 13 species of primate, and 420 species of birds (Mackinnon et al, 1997). However, also like Sumatra, widespread logging, which began under the period of European colonization and has accelerated in the last 40 years, and the growing palm oil industry and related forest conversion, has seen the islands forest cover decrease by around 50% (Matthews, 2002). It is now estimated that the area under concession for logging and oil palm cultivation in Borneo is larger than that of the remaining forest (Rijsken & Meijaard, 1999).

The most recent estimates put the population of Bornean orangutans at around 55,000 (Wich et al, 2008), and the species, better known and generally better studied than its Sumatran cousin, has benefited from both a strong international NGO presence, and Borneo's series of national parks, which, despite massive incursions and continued threats, today harbor significant populations of orangutans. In 2016, the IUCN reclassified the Bornean orangutan as "critically endangered" primarily due to the continued degradation of habitat (IUCN Redlist, 2016).

[...]

Human-Orangutan Conflict

The conflict between humans and wildlife is one of the greatest threats to the survival of endangered species throughout the world, and while this conflict is not a new phenomenon, and our species' relationship with the world's other animals has been marked by intense competition for as long as humans have walked the earth, dwindling resources and a soaring human population has seen it become an increasing focus of conservation efforts.

[...]

Throughout the islands of Borneo and Sumatra, prime orangutan habitat has been converted to logging concessions, pulp, and paper plantations, mines and agricultural plantations, particularly for the cultivation of rubber and palm oil. Such habitat loss and fragmentation has been devastating to orangutan populations, with the acceleration of palm oil plantations having dramatically increased incidents of direct conflict between orangutans and humans (Yuwono et al, 2007), as orangutans are forced out of degraded forest into plantations in search of food. Although tolerance to orangutan crop raiding varies from plantation to plantation, increasing human-orangutan conflicts ultimately results in an increase in orangutan killing, and often an increase in poaching for the illegal pet trade (Hadisiswoyo, 2008). It has been observed that poaching and trade is particularly common in areas where plantations are being developed, and, despite being legally protected in Indonesia, orangutans are increasingly being regarded as crop-raiding pests, and being illegally killed (Hadisiswoyo, 2008).

In Sumatra, which has one of the highest deforestation rates in the tropics (Campbell-Smith et al, 2011), forest conversion and a corresponding increase in human-orangutan conflict has been severe, particularly in areas around the Gunung Leuser National Park in North Sumatra, where orangutans have been forced in to fragmented patches of forests surrounded by agricultural

---

Humpback Whales: A Success Story

Federal authorities took most humpback whales off the endangered species list Tuesday, saying their numbers have recovered through international efforts to protect the giant mammals.

Known for their acrobatic leaps from the sea and complex singing patterns, humpback whales were nearly hunted to extinction for their oil and meat by industrial-sized whaling ships well through the middle of the 20th century. But the species has been bouncing back since an international ban on commercial whaling took effect in 1966.

The moratorium on whaling remains in effect, despite the new classifications.

The National Marine Fisheries Service said it first had evidence to indicate there were 14 distinct populations of humpback whales around the world. It then said nine of these populations have recovered to the point where they no longer need Endangered Species Act Protections. These include whales that winter in Hawaii, the West Indies and Australia.

"Today's news is a true ecological success story," Eileen Sobeck, assistant administrator for fisheries at the National Oceanic and Atmospheric Administration, said in a statement.

The whales will continue to be protected under other federal laws, including the Marine Mammal Protection Act. Vessels will continue to

---

plantations (Hadisiswoyo, 2008). Studies have shown that individual orangutans can eat around 300 young oil palms in just two days, at a cost of around $2 per tree (Hadisiswoyo, 2008), a huge economic loss for an agricultural farmer in that part of the world.

To mitigate these problems, OURF, working with our partners in Sumatra, has established the Mobile Education and Conservation Unit (MECU), a program aimed at educating local people about orangutan issues and reducing conflict, by improving agro-forestry techniques and current farming methods. The work, however, is not easy. Although human-wildlife conflicts are present in nearly all rural villages, the form they take, the species involved and the village's perception of the problem varies.

have to stay a specific distance away from humpback whales in Hawaii and Alaska waters.

An estimated 11,000 humpback whales breed in Hawaii waters each winter and migrate to Alaska to feed during the summer, the fisheries service said.

But an environmentalist group said the protections should stay in place.

Humpbacks that breed in Central America in the winter and feed off California and the Pacific Northwest in the summer are among those that will remain on the endangered list.

Whales that breed off Mexico and feed off California, the Pacific Northwest and Alaska will be listed as threatened. There are about 3,200 of the whales in this group, which is only about half of what scientists previously thought, Nammack said.

The different classifications mean that Alaska's whales will be a mix.

In addition to whales that breed in Hawaii and Mexico, Alaska also gets whales that spend the winter in waters around Okinawa and the Philippines. These whales, called the Western North Pacific population, are endangered.

Humpback whales are also found along eastern coasts of the U.S. and Canada. These whales, which winter in the West Indies, are not being listed as endangered. They number about 10,000, the fisheries service said.

"Most Humpback Whales Off Endangered List In 'Ecological Success Story,'" NPR, September 7, 2016.

During a two year study in to orangutan-human conflicts in two districts in North Sumatra, between February 2007 to February 2009, researchers discovered that in one of the districts, Batang Serangan, which contained an orangutan population of 16 individuals, 56% of survey respondents reported problems with orangutans, and orangutans were ranked as the third most frequent crop pest entering farmlands, being the fourth most destructive. They were also regarded as the most feared species in the district (Campbell-Smith, 2010).

In the second district, Sidiangkat, which contained an orangutan population of 134 individuals, there were, however, no reports of crop raiding orangutans, with wild boar, pig-tailed macaques, and civet cats being the most problematic species. However, like Batang Serangan, orangutans were again considered the most feared animal in this district (Campbell-Smith, 2010).

Throughout both districts, 97% of respondents claimed to have never caught an orangutan, and 83% knew that such an act would be illegal. However, of the 3% that claimed to have caught an orangutan, 64% said it was in retribution for crop raiding, with 18% saying it was to keep it as a pet, 14% catching it for food, and 4% saying it was caught to be sold in the pet trade (Campbell-Smith, 2010).

The study also found that local people's tolerance of orangutans, and most likely other wildlife, was highly influenced by how much of a threat they considered them to be to their personal safety, with 29% of respondents claiming that orangutans were dangerous, with 31% stating this was because of their large size, 26% stating it was their ability to chase and capture humans, 13% saying they could bite a person, 12% of respondents highlighting their aggressive nature, and 18% attributing it to longstanding local legends (Campbell-Smith, 2010). Although respondents most often showed benign tolerance toward orangutans, this changed if there was ever a threat to themselves or their families' safety, when a more direct approach would be taken to remove the orangutan from their plantation or village. Although 98% of respondents agreed that orangutans should be protected under Indonesian law, many felt that they did not get the support they needed from local forestry officials, village heads or NGO's to deal with the problem (Campbell-Smith, 2010).

These findings were corroborated by a separate survey in 7 nearby villages surrounding the Gunung Leuser National Park, which found that local people perceived orangutans as crop raiders, and that, while they were not the most problematic, they were the most feared, considered dangerous due to their large size. While local people had concerns about the amount of fruit such a large-bodied animal could potentially consume, a large number were still emphatic in their belief that orangutans were a protected species, and that their protection was important, and although farmers in this survey took more active measures to protect their crops, this usually amounted to shouting and throwing, with shooting an infrequently used method (Hadisiswoyo, 2008).

Surprisingly, most respondents in this survey reported that orangutans do not raid palm oil plantations, and were instead most problematic in areas with rubber and jackfruit trees. While this is possibly due to Sumatran orangutans being strictly arboreal, and not being able to move from tree to tree in palm oil plantations without descending to the ground, it nevertheless highlights the variations in orangutan behavior from place to place.

Farmers in this area also highlighted the difficulties in driving orangutans from their plantations, partly because of their known protected status and a desire not to get in to trouble, but also because the orangutans isolated status meant driving an orangutan from one plantation would simply force them on to another, most likely owned by a neighboring farmer. Unless orangutans could be relocated to a wild area, any dispersal methods would be considered a selfish act against another farmer (Hadisiswoyo, 2008).

Addressing these issues, and balancing the needs of wildlife with the needs and reasonable expectation of local people, is one of the most complex and difficult aspects of orangutan conservation. Halting the conversion of tropical forests to plantations must remain the priority, but in areas already degraded, local people need stronger support from local forestry officials and NGO's to deal with orangutans and other crop raiders on their plantations, and education and improved farming techniques to make better use of, and to better protect, their farms. It is hoped that with continued research and OURF's developing conservation and education initiatives the incidence of conflict can be reduced, and the orangutans and people of Sumatra and Borneo can co-exist peacefully.

In Costa Rica Research in Tropical Reforestation Is Working

Dr. Karen D. Holl

In the following viewpoint Dr. Karen D. Holl presents the results of research done on land reforestation studies. Dr. Holl maintains that certain strategies work best and can be maintained economically. Dr. Holl's research has extended beyond her original research site, proving beneficial to other tropical areas. Dr. Karen D. Holl is a professor of environmental studies at the University of California Santa Cruz and in research focuses on how ecosystems recover from human disturbance.

As you read, consider the following questions:

1. According to the author, what is one of the most common ways to restore deforested land?
2. Where is Dr. Holl's original research site, and where has it expanded to as explained by the viewpoint?
3. What strategy did Dr. Holl discover worked best for reforestation?

"Planting Tree Islands to Restore Tropical Forest," by Dr. Karen D. Holl, Karen D. Holl, January 21, 2015. Reprinted by permission.

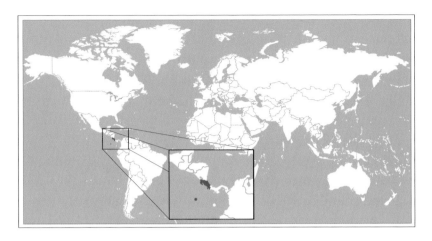

When one thinks about forest restoration likely the first thing that comes to mind is planting trees. This isn't the only way to restore deforested land, but it is one of the most common. When we plant trees, we usually plant them in rows. But think about what a naturally recovering forest looks like in an area that was previously used for agriculture or livestock grazing. After a few years this land will typically sport scattered patches of young trees and shrubs in a disorganized, yet more natural pattern. As a restoration ecologist, I have thought a great deal about how to design land recovery strategies that are both cost effective and as similar to natural processes as possible. Would planting trees in patches or islands rather than in systematic rows produce a more heterogeneous, resilient system? Could we reduce restoration costs by requiring fewer seedlings to grow, plant, and maintain?

Over a decade ago, my colleague Zak Zahawi and I, along with the help of many students and field assistants, began an experiment in a premontane forest in southern Costa Rica to answer just these questions. We established 16 restoration sites and tested three restoration approaches at each site: "Natural regeneration" where the forest was left to recover without any human intervention; "plantation" style tree planting where the entire area was planted with tree seedlings in even rows; and "island" style planting where just over a quarter of the area was planted with three different sizes of tree seedling clumps or "islands." To evaluate the effect on recovery rates of having intact forests nearby, we established our experimental sites in locations with different degrees of surrounding forest cover. Some sites were situated in the middle of agricultural lands while others were adjacent to the largest forest remnants in the region. We hoped to learn not just whether different planting regimes can affect forest recovery, but also the effect of different locations for planting. In other words, is it more important how you restore, or where?

We have been following the recovery of our different test sites for almost 15 years by collecting data on seed dispersal, soil nutrients, seedling establishment, understory and canopy cover, bird and bat presence, mycorrhizae, and insects. Tropical forests are highly diverse, and rates of recovery can vary greatly depending on the type of recovering forest, the intensity of past land-uses, and whether there are isolated trees or remnant forests nearby to serve as seed sources. In this study our aim was not to plant the full diversity of trees found in the forest but rather to provide a diverse vertical structure (e.g., vegetation of different heights) that could attract a diversity of birds and bats and shade out the tall pasture grasses that perpetually compete with tree seedlings for light and nutrients. Birds and bats are key to the recovery of a tropic forest, as they disperse the majority of tree seeds. Only through such faunal seed dispersal can a restoration site establish a diversity of forest plants.

What we have found so far is striking: planting tree islands is cheaper than and as effective as traditional plantation-style restoration in accelerating the recovery of deforested land. Moreover, recovery in tree island treatments appears to better simulate natural processes.

What did we find exactly? First, we found that plantation and tree island restoration outperform natural regeneration treatments with more than double the amount of seed dispersal and four times the number of seedlings established, two key indicators of restoration success. Second, we found that there is a critical minimum size

(~100 m²) for tree islands to outperform natural regeneration, particularly for them to effectively enhance bird activity, dispersal of forest tree seeds, and tree seedling establishment. Third, we found that planted islands expand in size over time due to both tree growth and new seedling recruitment at their edges. We also found that islands are expanding and coalescing at some of our sites. Finally, we found that planting tree islands results in greater canopy heterogeneity than the plantation-style approach.

Results to date also suggest that the amount of surrounding forest cover does not strongly influence animal-dispersed seed rain and native woody species establishment during the first decade of succession. For now it seem seems that restoration strategy is more important than site location within a landscape. But we anticipate that surrounding forest cover will have a progressively stronger effect on forest recovery as succession proceeds and a greater diversity of plants and animals colonize the sites.

We now think that the tree island restoration approach holds promise as an innovative restoration strategy for some systems, particularly where natural recovery rates are slow, large areas need to be restored, or restoration resources are limited. The irregular, tree island planting strategy does offer some logistical challenges over plantation planting, as most post-planting site maintenance (e.g., controlling competitive grasses) is done along even lines in planted forests. The farmers in our region were certainly more accustomed to this approach and this resulted in some trees being damaged in the island test sites during routine clearing of grasses. The most appropriate restoration approach at any site will depend on the goals and constraints of a project. Nevertheless, our findings show promising results and decreased cost from this new strategy— something that should be hard to ignore in most places attempting large restoration without large budgets.

We are now testing this approach at additional locations. Two years ago, we worked with Pedro Brancalion, at the University of São Paulo, to set up a study comparing tree island plantings and planting in strips of trees alternating with open unplanted areas in the Atlantic forest of Brazil. We're also working with collaborators in Colombia on a tree island planting study there. You can visit our website (http://www.holl-lab.com/tropical-forests.html) for selected publications and a broader discussion behind the science of this study. You can watch a 7-minute video on our project at https://www.youtube.com/watch?v=QPZIIMZrIqQ.

AUTHOR'S NOTE: This is a revised and updated version of a 2015 post as part of the IUCN Science and Practice of Forest Landscape Restoration blog series (https://www.iucn.org/content/forest-island-effect).

Periodical and Internet Sources Bibliography

The following articles have been selected to supplement the diverse views presented in this chapter.

Molly Bergen, "Stopping Deforestation in the Amazon by 2020? It's Possible," Humanature, August 10, 2016, https://blog. conservation.org/2016/08/stopping-deforestation-in-the-amazon-by-2020-its-possible/

Sara Kaiser, "DIY Biosecurity: 5 Ways to Prevent Spread of Invasive Species," Island Conservation, February 27, 2017, https://www. islandconservation.org/stop-spread-invasive-species/

Giovanni Ortolani, "Brazil Has the Tools to Stop Amazon Deforestation Now: Report," Mongabay, May 18, 2018, https:// news.mongabay.com/2018/05/brazil-has-the-tools-to-end-amazon-deforestation-now-report/

Matt Palmer, "Discovering Urban Biodiversity," The Nature of Cities, August 14, 2012, https://www.thenatureofcities.com/2012/08/14/ discovering-urban-biodiversity/

Erin Spencer, "3 Easy Ways to Stop Invasive Species," The Ocean Conservancy, March 2, 2017, https://oceanconservancy.org/ blog/2017/03/02/3-easy-ways-to-stop-invasive-species/

Stanford University, "Researchers Rethink 'Natural' Habitat for Wildlife," Science Daily, April 18, 2014, https://www.sciencedaily. com/releases/2014/04/140418161437.htm

Jonathan Watts, "Stop Biodiversity Loss or We Could Face Our Own Extinction, Warns UN," *The Guardian*, November 6, 2018, https://www.theguardian.com/environment/2018/nov/03/stop-biodiversity-loss-or-we-could-face-our-own-extinction-warns-un

Bob Yirka, "Field Study Suggests Islands and Forest Fragments Are Not as Alike as Thought," Phys.org, April 17, 2014, https://phys. org/news/2014-04-field-islands-forest-fragments-alike.html

For Further Discussion

Chapter 1

1. Compare the strategies that Mozambique and Australia could use to stop further loss of biodiversity in their countries?
2. What are the similarities and differences used by Mozambique, Australia, Ecuador, and China to promote biodiversity and conservation in their countries?

Chapter 2

1. Would Kelvin Thompson and Kumi Naidoo agree with each other's ideas on how to protect biodiversity, and why?
2. How might habitat fragmentation figure into biodiversity plans for farmers? Explain your answer using specific examples from this chapter's viewpoints.

Chapter 3

1. How do climate change, loss of biodiversity, and nuclear weapons pose a global threat to the survival of humanity?
2. How does global homogenization and the introduction of exotic animal and plant species contribute to the loss of biodiversity?

Chapter 4

1. Should zoos be encouraged and supported? Why or why not?
2. Why might poorer countries be tempted to use biodiversity offsets?

Organizations to Contact

The editors have compiled the following list of organizations concerned with the issues debated in this book. The descriptions are derived from materials provided by the organizations. All have publications or information available for interested readers. The list was compiled on the date of publication of the present volume; the information provided here may change. Be aware that many organizations take several weeks or longer to respond to inquiries, so allow as much time as possible.

African Wildlife Foundation (AWF)
1100 New Jersey Avenue SE, Suite 900
Washington, DC 20003
(202) 939-3333
email: africanwildlife@awf.org
website: www.awf.org/

The AWF works to protect Africa's wildlife, and to ensure that both wildlife and wild lands can thrive in modern Africa. Read about this issue on the organization's site and sign up to receive a newsletter to stay current with breaking news and information.

American Cetacean Society (ACS)
PO Box 51691
Pacific Grove, CA 93950
(310) 549-6279
email: ACSoffice@ACSonline.org
website: www.acsonline.org/

The ACS is the first conservation group in the world dedicated to whales, porpoises, and dolphins. The agency is dedicated to bringing education, and current information about conservation of this animal group through research by its network of scientists and experts in the United States and around the world.

Center for Biological Diversity
PO Box 710
Tucson, AZ 85702-0710
(520) 623-5252
email: center@biologicaldiversity.org
website: https://www.biologicaldiversity.org/

The Center for Biological Diversity believes that humans are deeply connected to all living things on Earth. Their mission is to secure biodiversity by protecting all wild animals and plants big or small. The agency maintains a wide range of publications, media and programs to further its mission.

Conservation International (CI)
2011 Crystal Drive, Suite 600
Arlington, VA 22202
(800) 429-5660
website: www.conservation.org

Recognizing humanity's dependence on the natural world, CI is working to build a prosperous, productive and healthy planet. There are many resources on this site including the ability to sign up for news delivered into your inbox about the latest issues in conservation.

Earth Law Center
249 East 118th Street, Suite 3B
New York, NY 10035
(646)833- 8521
email: info@earthlaw.org
website: www.earthlawcenter.org/

The Earth Law Center is an organization that describes itself as a champion of nature. They help communities around the world by putting new laws into place that protect the environment. Read about their work on this site. Get ideas how to do your share in their book, *Three Solutions to Save Planet A*.

EO Wilson Foundation
300 Blackwell Street, Suite 102
Durham, NC 27701
(984) 219-2270
email: info@eowilsonfoundation.org
website: https://eowilsonfoundation.org/

The EO Wilson Foundation is guided by the inspiration from Edward O. Wilson, award-winning writer, speaker, scientist and environmental champion. The foundation's mission is to educate the public about biodiversity so that people all over will become stewards of the land.

International Union for Conservation of Nature (IUCN)
1630 Connecticut Avenue NW, Suite 300
Washington, DC 20009
(202) 387-4826
email: deborah.good@iucn.org
website: www.iucn.org/

IUCN is the world's largest network of governmental and private organizations dedicated to environmental concerns. The organization oversees conservation projects and meets every four years at the IUCN World Conservation Congress.

National Wildlife Federation (NWF)
11100 Wildlife Center Drive
Weston, VA 20190
(800) 822-9919
email: Use form on contact page
website: www.nwf.org/

The NWF has a mission and a strategic plan to increase the populations of fish and wildlife in America and to make sure our natural heritage thrives into the future. Get information on this site for people of all ages to help understand, enjoy, and cultivate America's natural resources.

Ocean Conservancy
1300 19th Street, NW, 8th Floor
Washington, DC 20036
(800) 519-1541
email: Check links on contact page.
website: https://oceanconservancy.org/

The Ocean Conservancy wants to inspire people to make a difference when it comes to protecting the world's oceans. They advocate against ocean trash, overfishing of the oceans and acidification of ocean waters. Get informed and become active by reading their articles on the blog and newsroom.

Rainforest Trust
7078 Airlie Road
Warrenton, VA 20187
(800) 456-4930
email: Use form on contact page.
website: www.rainforesttrust.org/

The Rainforest Trust is interested in the conservation and biodiversity of rainforests around the world. The agency purchases tracts of rainforest that are vulnerable to destruction thereby saving the animal and plant species native to the area.

World Wildlife Fund (WWF)
1250 24th Street, N.W.
Washington, DC 20037
(202) 293-4800
email: See contact page
website: www.worldwildlife.org/

The World Wildlife Fund is a global organization with a mission to reduce threats to biodiversity around the world and conserve nature.

Bibliography of Books

Leslie Anthony, *The Aliens Among Us: How Invasive Species are Transforming the Planet-and Ourselves*, New Haven, CT: Yale University Press, 2017.

Nicola Davies, *Many: The Diversity of Life on Earth*, Somerville, MA: Candlewick Press, 2017

Paul R. Ehrlich, *Hope on Earth: A Conversation*, Chicago, IL: University of Chicago Press, 2014.

Kim Masters Evans, *Endangered Species: Protecting Biodiversity*, Farmington Hills, MI: Gale Cengage Learning, 2016.

Dante B. Fenolio, *Life in the Dark: Illuminating Biodiversity in the Shadowy Haunts of Planet Earth*, Baltimore, MD: John Hopkins University Press, 2016.

Alexandros Gasparatos and KJ Willis, *Biodiversity in the Green Economy*, London: Routledge, 2017.

Jane Goodall, *Hope for Animals and Their World: How Endangered Species and Being Rescued from the Brink*, New York: NY, Grand Central Publishing, 2009.

Rachel Ignotofsky, *The Wondrous Workings of Planet Earth: Understanding Our World and Its Ecosystems*, Berkeley: CA, Ten Speed Press, 2018.

James B. MacKinnon, *The Once and Future World: Nature As It Was, As It Is, As It Could Be*, New York: NY, Houghton Mifflin Harcourt, 2013.

Reeser Manley, *The Life in Your Garden: Gardening for Biodiversity*, Thomaston: ME, Tilbury House Publications, 2016.

Richard G. Pearson, *Driven to Extinction: The Impact of Climate Change on Biodiversity*, New York: NY, Sterling, 2011.

Helga Schier, *Endangered Oceans*, New York: NY, Greenhaven Press, 2014.

Fernando Vidal and Nelia Dias, *Endangerment, Biodiversity and Culture,* New York: Routledge, 2016.

Edward O. Wilson, *Half-Earth: Our Planet's Fight for Life,* New York: NY, W. W. Norton & Co., 2016.

Index